Quick Meals

JENNY FANSHAW, ANNETTE FORREST

Quick Meals

OVER **140** DELICIOUS RECIPES

Reader's
Digest

THE READER'S DIGEST ASSOCIATION, INC.
NEW YORK, NEW YORK / MONTREAL / SYDNEY / SINGAPORE

A READER'S DIGEST BOOK

This edition published by
The Reader's Digest Association, Inc.,
by arrangement with McRae Books Srl

Quick Meals was created and produced by
McRae Publishing Ltd, London
info@mcraebooks.com

FOR MCRAE BOOKS
Project Director: Anne McRae
Art Director: Marco Nardi
Photography: Brent Parker Jones
Photographic Art Direction: Neil Hargreaves
Texts: Jenny Fanshaw, Annette Forrest
Food Styling: Lee Blaycock, Neil Hargreaves
Layouts: Aurora Granata
Prepress: Filippo Delle Monache, Davide Gasparri

FOR READER'S DIGEST
U.S. Project Editor: Andrea Chesman
Canadian Project Editor: Pamela Chichinskas
Australian Project Editor: Annette Carter
Copy Editor: Emily Bigelow
Senior Art Director: George McKeon
Executive Editor, Trade Publishing: Dolores York
Associate Publisher, Trade Publishing: Rosanne McManus
President and Publisher, Trade Publishing: Harold Clarke

ISBN 978-1-60652-248-6

We are committed to both the quality of our products and
the service we provide to our customers. We value your
comments, so please feel free to contact us.

The Reader's Digest Association, Inc.
Adult Trade Publishing
44 S. Broadway
White Plains, NY 10601

NOTE TO OUR READERS
Eating eggs or egg whites that are not completely cooked
poses the possibility of salmonella food poisoning. The risk
is greater for pregnant women, the elderly, the very young,
and persons with impaired immune systems. If you are
concerned about salmonella, you can use reconstituted
powdered egg whites or pasteurized eggs.

For more Reader's Digest products and information, visit
our website:
    www.rd.com (in the United States)
    www.readersdigest.ca (in Canada)
    www.readersdigest.com.au (in Australia)
    www.readersdigest.com.nz (in New Zealand)

Printed in China

1 3 5 7 9 10 8 6 4 2

The level of difficulty for each recipe is given on a scale
from 1 (easy) to 2 (fairly easy)

CONTENTS

INTRODUCTION

This book is dedicated to busy people who enjoy simple, stylish food that can be prepared with a minimum of fuss and in less time than it takes to get takeout. From comfort food like Potatoes Stuffed with Beans and Spaghetti with Cherry Tomatoes, to gourmet offerings such as Veal Saltimbocca and Chocolate Fudge and Amaretti Sundaes, we have selected more than 140 dishes from a mixture of homestyle cooking and popular world cuisines such as Italian, Mexican, and Chinese. We have streamlined their preparation and cooking times so they can all be prepared in 30 minutes or less, from start to finish.

The recipes have been organized into nine chapters, from Snacks and Starters to Desserts. We have tried to choose dishes that are complete in themselves and hearty enough to be served on their own. Many of the salads and soups include serving suggestions for different types of bread or croutons so you can whip up a healthy and satisfying light meal in 30 minutes or less. But you can also combine the recipes to prepare a more substantial family meal of two or three courses, all in less than an hour.

We believe that the key to preparing tasty food quickly, without sacrificing either flavor or nutritional value, lies in the use of fresh, high-quality ingredients. Quick food doesn't need to be based on canned or prepackaged foodstuffs—a handful of garden-fresh vegetables seared in a wok with vegetable oil and a spice or two, then sprinkled with fresh herbs and served over rice or noodles makes a delectable and healthy meal. We have included several Asian favorites of this type. Also included are several Italian dishes that can be prepared easily and quickly.

Classics like risotto and spaghetti are among the many recipes featured in the chapters on Pasta and Grains.

Fish and seafood are high in protein and other nutritional values and are quick to cook. Try our Tuna Steaks with Oranges and Capers (see page 182) or Parmesan-crumbed Baked Salmon (see page 192), or any of the other recipes in the Seafood chapter. You will find more ideas for protein-packed meals in the chapters on Poultry and Meat. To finish, we have included a dozen recipes for desserts, from puddings and soufflés to Chocolate Tarts and quick-fix Tiramisù.

To help you plan your meals, each recipe includes preparation and cooking times. We have also graded the recipes either 1 or 2 for difficulty (1=easy and 2=fairly easy), with almost all falling into the first category.

Within you will find a full range of dazzling ideas for every occasion, from impressive meals when you are entertaining, to simpler dishes you can fix for friends and family on busy weeknights or lazy weekends.

SNACKS AND STARTERS

SMOKED SALMON DIP

Process the smoked salmon, cream cheese, lemon juice, capers, and dill in a food processor until smooth. Season with salt and pepper. • Spoon the dip into a serving bowl, garnish with the dill, and serve with crackers.

5   ounces (150 g) smoked salmon (or smoked trout)

1   cup (250 g) light cream cheese, at room temperature

2   tablespoons freshly squeezed lemon juice

1^1/$_2$ tablespoons salt-cured capers, rinsed

2   tablespoons finely chopped fresh dill + a sprig to garnish

Salt and freshly ground black pepper

Crackers, to serve

Preparation: 10 minutes

Serves: 4
Level: 1

■■■ *Serve this dip with predinner drinks. It is great with thin, crisp crackers but can also be served with potato chips (crisps), corn chips, or thin slices of toasted bread.*

BACON AND MUSHROOM PIZZA

Preheat the oven to 450°F (230°C/gas 8). • Sauté the bacon and mushrooms in the oil in a large frying pan over medium heat until the mushrooms are softened, about 5 minutes. • Remove from the heat and set aside. • Spread the pizza crust with the tomato paste. • Top with the mushrooms, bacon, shallots, and mozzarella. • Bake for 12–15 minutes, until golden brown and crisp. • Top with the arugula and season with salt and pepper. • Serve hot.

3   slices bacon, coarsely chopped

8   ounces (250 g) mushrooms, thinly sliced

1   tablespoon extra-virgin olive oil

1   12-inch (30-cm) store-bought pizza crust

1/4 cup (60 g) tomato paste

2   shallots, thinly sliced

1/2 cup (125 g) freshly grated mozzarella cheese

1   cup (30 g) arugula (rocket)

Salt and freshly ground black pepper

Preparation: 10 minutes
Cooking: 17–20 minutes

Serves: 1–2
Level: 1

HAM, CHEESE, AND AVOCADO QUESADILLAS

20

Lay out the tortillas on a clean work surface. • Place a slice of ham on each tortilla and spread with the mayonnaise. • Arrange the avocado, cheese, and arugula evenly over one half of the tortilla. • Season with salt and pepper. • Fold the tortillas in half. • Heat a large frying pan over medium heat. • Spray the tortillas with the oil. • Cook on each side until golden and crisp, for 2–3 minutes. • Serve warm.

4 **large flour tortillas or Mexican wraps**

4 **large slices ham**

2 **tablespoons mayonnaise**

1 **avocado, pitted (stoned) and thinly sliced**

8 **slices Swiss cheese**

2 **cups (60 g) arugula (rocket)**

Salt and freshly ground black pepper

Olive oil spray

Preparation: 10 minutes
Cooking: 4–6 minutes

Serves: 4
Level: 1

SAUSAGE AND TABBOULEH WRAPS

Put the bulgur in a bowl and cover with cold water. Let stand for 25 minutes. • Sauté the sausages in 1 tablespoon of oil in a large frying pan over medium heat until cooked, about 10 minutes. • Remove from the heat and set aside. • Squeeze the excess moisture out of the bulgur and put into a bowl. • Stir in the parsley, mint, tomato, onion, remaining oil, and lemon juice. Season with salt and pepper. • Cut the sausages into long, thick slices. • Lay out the flat breads on a clean surface. • Spread evenly with the hummus and top with the tabbouleh and sausage. • Roll up carefully. Cut each wrap in half and serve.

1/4 cup (60 g) fine- or medium-grain bulgur

6 spicy sausages, such as pepperoni

2 tablespoons extra-virgin olive oil

1 cup (30 g) finely chopped fresh parsley

2 tablespoons finely chopped fresh mint

1 large tomato, finely chopped

1/2 small red onion, finely chopped

1/4 cup (60 ml) freshly squeezed lemon juice

Salt and freshly ground black pepper

4 Lebanese flat breads, pita breads, or flour wraps

2/3 cup (150 g) hummus

Preparation: 25 minutes
Cooking: 12 minutes

Serves: 4
Level: 1

TURKEY, CAMEMBERT, AND CRANBERRY BAGELS

24

Place the bagel halves on a clean surface. • Spread each half with the cream cheese. Top evenly with the turkey, Camembert, cranberry sauce, and pea shoots. • Season with salt and pepper and serve.

4	bagels, cut in half
1/3	cup (90 ml) cream cheese
8	slices roasted or seasoned cooked turkey breast
8	thin slices Camembert cheese
1/3	cup (90 ml) cranberry sauce
1	cup (60 g) pea shoots or snow pea sprouts
	Salt and freshly ground black pepper

 Preparation: 10 minutes

Serves: 4
Level: 1

■■■ *If preferred, toast the bagels lightly before assembling the sandwiches. Serve while still warm from toasting.*

SWEET AND SPICY CHICKEN WRAPS

Mix the chicken, mayonnaise, and sweet chili sauce in a bowl. • Lay the flat breads out on a clean surface. • Divide the chicken mixture, cucumber, tomatoes, carrot, and lettuce evenly among the flat breads. Season with salt and pepper. • Roll up the bread and cut in half. Serve.

4 cups (400 g) shredded cooked chicken

1/3 cup (90 ml) mayonnaise

2 tablespoons Thai sweet chili sauce

4 Lebanese flat breads, pita breads, or flour wraps

1 cucumber, thinly sliced

2 tomatoes, finely chopped

1 large carrot, finely grated

2 cups (100 g) finely shredded lettuce

Salt and freshly ground black pepper

Preparation: 5 minutes

Serves: 4
Level: 1

TUNA PASTRY PIES

Preheat the oven to 375°F (190°C/gas 5).
• Lightly spray six muffin cups with olive
oil. • Place the phyllo pastry on a clean
work surface. • Lightly spray one sheet
with olive oil, fold in half lengthwise, and
spray again. • Fold again to form a
square. Repeat with the remaining phyllo
and olive oil. • Place the pastry squares
in the prepared muffin pans. • Mix the
tuna, arugula, scallions, eggs, and cream
in a large bowl. Season with salt and
pepper. • Spoon the mixture evenly into
the phyllo cases. • Bake for about
20 minutes, until golden brown
and crisp. • Serve hot.

Olive oil spray

6 sheets frozen phyllo
(filo) pastry, thawed

2 cups (400 g)
canned tuna,
drained and flaked

1/2 cup (15 g) finely
chopped arugula
(rocket)

4 scallions (green
onions), thinly sliced

5 large eggs,
lightly beaten

1/3 cup (90 ml) light
(single) cream

Salt and freshly
ground black pepper

 Preparation: 10 minutes
Cooking: 20 minutes

Serves: 4–6
Level: 1

MARJORAM BLINIS WITH PROSCIUTTO

Beat the flour, baking powder, sugar, salt, egg yolks, butter, marjoram, and milk in a large bowl until smooth. • Beat the egg whites in a large bowl with a mixer at high speed until stiff peaks form. • In a separate bowl, beat the cream with a mixer at high speed until stiff. • Use a large rubber spatula to fold the beaten whites and cream into the batter. • Heat a large frying pan over medium heat. Brush the pan with a little butter. • Drop tablespoons of the batter into the frying pan. Cook in batches until golden brown on both sides. • Transfer the cooked blinis to a serving dish. • Top each blini with slices of melon and prosciutto. • Serve warm.

1^1/$_2$ cups (225 g) all-purpose (plain) flour

2 teaspoons baking powder

1 teaspoon sugar

^{1}/$_2$ teaspoon salt

2 large eggs, separated

3 tablespoons butter, melted

1 tablespoon finely chopped fresh marjoram

1 cup (250 ml) milk, hot

^{1}/$_4$ cup (60 ml) heavy (double) cream

1 small ripe cantaloupe (rock) melon, peeled, seeded, and cut into thin wedges

4 ounces (125 g) prosciutto (Parma ham)

Preparation: 10 minutes

Cooking: 5 minutes

Serves: 4–6

Level: 2

CROSTONI WITH PROSCIUTTO, PEACH, AND PECORINO

32

Spread each slice of toast lightly with butter. • Place a slice of prosciutto on top. Cover with the peach slices and arugula. Sprinkle with the chives and top with the pecorino. • Season generously with pepper, if liked, and serve.

4 large slices firm-textured bread, toasted

2 tablespoons butter

4 large thin slices prosciutto (Parma ham)

1 large ripe peach, peeled, pitted, and thinly sliced

1 cup (30 g) arugula (rocket)

1 tablespoon finely chopped fresh chives

2 ounces (60 g) pecorino cheese, thinly sliced

Freshly ground black pepper (optional)

Preparation: 5 minutes

Serves: 4
Level: 1

■■■ *You may already know that a crostino (plural "crostini") is a classic Italian appetizer made from day-old bread, usually toasted, and then spread with various toppings, such as sliced tomatoes, Parmesan, olive or chicken liver pâté, among others. A crostoni is just a larger version of the same thing.*

YELLOW AND RED TOMATO BRUSCHETTA

34

Mix the tomatoes, onion, basil, garlic, olive oil, and balsamic vinegar in a medium bowl. Season with salt and pepper. • Cover with plastic wrap (cling film) and let stand for 20 minutes to let the flavor develop. • Cut the bread into ³⁄₄-inch (2-cm) slices. • Char-grill for 1–2 minutes on each side until toasted. • Spoon the tomato mixture over the bread and serve.

8	ounces (250 g) red tomatoes, coarsely chopped
8	ounces (250 g) yellow tomatoes, coarsely chopped
1	small red onion, finely chopped
2	tablespoons torn basil
1	clove garlic, finely chopped
2	tablespoons extra-virgin olive oil
1	tablespoon balsamic vinegar
	Salt and freshly ground black pepper
1	small loaf ciabatta bread or 1 crusty baguette (French loaf)

Preparation: 5 minutes + 20 minutes to stand
Cooking: 2–4 minutes

Serves: 4
Level: 1

■■■ *Bruschetta is a well-known Italian appetizer. In its simplest form, bruschetta consists of day-old bread, toasted, rubbed with garlic, and drizzled with extra-virgin olive oil. It can also be topped with tomatoes, cannellini beans, or spinach, among other things. Always remember to say the name correctly— it's pronounced "brusketta" (not brushetta)!*

SUN-DRIED TOMATO PESTO TOASTS

36

Preheat the oven to 350°F (180°C/gas 4). • Arrange the bread on baking sheets and drizzle with 1 tablespoon of olive oil. • Bake for 5 minutes on each side, until golden and crisp. • Arrange the toasts on a large serving platter. • Process the sun-dried tomatoes, remaining olive oil, capers, garlic, lemon zest, lemon juice, and thyme in a food processor until well blended. • Arrange the arugula leaves and sun-dried tomato pesto on top of the toasts. Top with the sliced mozzarella and serve.

1	crusty baguette (French loaf), thickly sliced
1/4	cup (60 ml) extra-virgin olive oil
3/4	cup (75 g) sun-dried tomatoes
2	tablespoons salt-cured capers, rinsed
2	cloves garlic, peeled
	Finely grated zest and juice of 1/2 lemon
1	tablespoon thyme leaves
1	cup (30 g) arugula (rocket) leaves
6	ounces (180 g) small fresh mozzarella balls (bocconcini), drained and sliced

Preparation: 15 minutes
Cooking: 10 minutes

Serves: 4
Level: 1

CHERRY TOMATO AND MOZZARELLA SKEWERS

Thread half a cherry tomato onto a wooden skewer. Follow with a leaf of basil and a mozzarella ball. Repeat until all the mozzarella, tomatoes, and basil have been used. • Place the skewers on a serving plate. • Sprinkle with the chives. Season with salt and pepper and drizzle with the oil.

12 cherry tomatoes, halved

24 leaves fresh basil

24 small fresh mozzarella balls (bocconcini)

1 tablespoon finely chopped fresh chives

Salt and freshly ground black pepper

1/4 cup (60 ml) extra-virgin olive oil

 Preparation: 15 minutes

Serves: 4
Level: 1

■■■ *This is a healthy snack that also can be served as a starter or light lunch. Its flavor depends on top-quality ingredients, so use the freshest mozzarella cheese and tomatoes and a good quality extra-virgin olive oil to drizzle.*

MEATBALLS WITH TOMATO SALSA

40

Mix the beef, scallions, parsley, tomato paste, bread crumbs, and egg in a large bowl until well blended. Season with salt and pepper. • Form the mixture into balls the size of walnuts. • Heat the oil until very hot in a large, deep frying pan. • Fry the meatballs in batches for 5–7 minutes, until golden brown all over. • Drain well on paper towels. Serve hot with the tomato salsa on the side.

1 pound (500 g) ground (minced) beef

3 scallions (green onions), finely chopped

2 tablespoons finely chopped fresh parsley

2 tablespoons tomato paste

3/4 cup (45 g) fresh bread crumbs

1 large egg, lightly beaten

Salt and freshly ground black pepper

1 cup (250 ml) olive oil, for frying

1 cup (250 ml) tomato salsa

Preparation: 10 minutes
Cooking: 5–7 minutes

Serves: 8–10
Level: 1

SALMON FISH CAKES

Mix the salmon, mashed potatoes, scallions, dill, and egg in a large bowl. Season with salt and pepper. • Shape the mixture into eight fish cakes. Lightly dust with the flour. • Fry the fish cakes in the oil in a large frying pan over medium heat until golden brown, 3–4 minutes on each side. • Drain on paper towels. Garnish with the lemon wedges and dill and serve hot.

2   cups (400 g) canned pink salmon, drained and flaked

1½ cups (350 g) leftover mashed potatoes

2   scallions (green onions), thinly sliced

2   tablespoons finely chopped dill + extra, to garnish

1   large egg, lightly beaten

Salt and freshly ground black pepper

2   tablespoons all-purpose (plain) flour

¼   cup (60 ml) extra-virgin olive oil

Lemon wedges, to serve

Preparation: 10 minutes
Cooking: 6–8 minutes

Serves: 4–6
Level: 1

SPICY POTATO WEDGES

Preheat the oven to 450°F (230°C/ gas 8). • Place the potato wedges in a microwave dish with the water. • Cover with plastic wrap (cling film) and microwave on high power for 5 minutes. • Drain the potatoes. • Place flour and Cajun seasoning in a plastic bag. • Add the potato wedges and toss well. • Place the wedges on a nonstick baking tray. Drizzle with the olive oil. • Bake for 15–20 minutes, until golden and crisp. • Serve hot with the sour cream and sweet chili sauce on the side.

4	large potatoes, scrubbed and cut into wedges
1	tablespoon water
2	tablespoons extra-virgin olive oil
1	tablespoon all-purpose (plain) flour
1	tablespoon Cajun seasoning
1/4	cup (60 ml) sour cream
1/4	cup (60 ml) Thai sweet chili sauce

Preparation: 5 minutes
Cooking: 20–25 minutes

Serves: 4
Level: 1

CHERRY TOMATO CLAFOUTIS

Preheat the oven to 400°F (200°C/ gas 6). • Grease four 1-cup (250-ml) ramekins or ovenproof dishes with oil. • Divide the tomatoes among the prepared ramekins and season with salt. • Beat the flour, eggs, milk, crème fraîche, and half the Parmesan in a large bowl until smooth. • Stir in the arugula. • Pour the mixture over the tomatoes. • Bake for 15 minutes, until set and golden brown on top. • Sprinkle with the remaining Parmesan. • Serve hot, with arugula on the side.

1 pound (500 g) cherry tomatoes, halved

Salt

2 tablespoons all-purpose (plain) flour

4 large eggs

Generous 1/3 cup (100 ml) milk

Generous 3/4 cup (200 g) crème fraîche or half-and-half

Generous 1/2 cup (70 g) freshly grated Parmesan cheese

2 cups (60 g) arugula (rocket) leaves, torn + extra to serve

Preparation: 10 minutes
Cooking: 15 minutes

Serves: 4
Level: 1

HUMMUS WITH TOMATOES AND OLIVES

Combine the garbanzo beans, tahini, garlic, vinegar, and $1/4$ cup (60 ml) of lemon juice in a food processor. Season with salt and pepper. • Process until smooth. If the mixture is too thick, add a little more lemon juice. • Mix the tomatoes, cucumber, olives, parsley, 1 tablespoon of oil, and 2 tablespoons of lemon juice in a large bowl. Season with salt and pepper. Toss well. • Spoon the hummus onto a serving plate and sprinkle with cayenne pepper. • Drizzle with a little oil. • Arrange the tomato salad in the center of the hummus and serve with the pita bread.

1   (14-ounce/400-g) can garbanzo beans (chick-peas), drained and rinsed

$1/3$ cup (90 ml) tahini

1   clove garlic, finely chopped

2   teaspoons white wine vinegar

6   tablespoons (90 ml) freshly squeezed lemon juice

Salt and freshly ground black pepper

2   tomatoes, diced

1   cucumber, diced

$1/3$ cup (30 g) pitted kalamata olives

1   tablespoon finely chopped fresh parsley

2   tablespoons extra-virgin olive oil

$1/8$ teaspoon cayenne pepper

Pita or Lebanese flat breads, to serve

Preparation: 15 minutes

Serves: 4
Level: 1

SALADS

SMOKED CHICKEN AND AVOCADO SALAD

For the salad: Toast the almonds in a large frying pan over medium heat for 3 minutes. • Remove from the heat and set aside. • Mix the chicken, avocado, cucumber, and lettuce in a large bowl. • For the dressing: Mix the lemon juice, olive oil, Dijon mustard, and sugar in a small bowl. Season with salt and pepper. • Drizzle over the salad and toss well.

Salad

1/4 cup (40 g) slivered almonds

1 pound (500 g) smoked chicken breasts, thinly sliced

2 small avocados, cut in half, pitted, and thinly sliced

1 cucumber, thinly sliced

1 head romaine lettuce, torn

Dressing

1/4 cup (60 ml) freshly squeezed lemon juice

2 tablespoons extra-virgin olive oil

1 tablespoon Dijon mustard

1 teaspoon superfine (caster) sugar

Salt and freshly ground black pepper

Preparation: 5 minutes

Cooking: 3 minutes

Serves: 4
Level: 1

PEAR AND BLUE CHEESE SALAD

Sauté the walnuts in 1 tablespoon of oil in a small frying pan over medium heat for 1 minute. • Add the honey and cook over low heat for 2 minutes. • Transfer to a small bowl. • Add the remaining olive oil and lemon juice. Let cool. • Mix the baby spinach, pears, and blue cheese in a large bowl. • Add the honeyed walnuts. Toss well and serve.

¹/₃	cup (50 g) walnuts
¹/₄	cup (60 ml) extra-virgin olive oil
1	tablespoon honey
2	tablespoons freshly squeezed lemon juice
5	ounces (150 g) baby spinach leaves
3	pears, halved, cored, and thinly sliced
8	ounces (250 g) blue cheese, such as Gorgonzola or Stilton, crumbled

Preparation: 15 minutes
Cooking: 3 minutes

Serves: 4
Level: 1

SPINACH AND FETA SALAD WITH CROUTONS

Sauté the bread cubes in 1 tablespoon of oil in a large frying pan over medium heat until crisp and golden, 5–7 minutes. • Drain well on paper towels. • Toss the sun-dried tomatoes, spinach, and feta in a large salad bowl. Drizzle with the remaining oil and white wine vinegar. Season with salt and pepper. • Add the croutons. Toss well and serve.

1/2 small baguette (French loaf), cut into small cubes

3 tablespoons extra-virgin olive oil

5 ounces (150 g) sun-dried tomatoes in oil, drained

5 ounces (150 g) baby spinach leaves

5 ounces (150 g) feta cheese, thinly sliced

1 tablespoon white wine vinegar

Salt and freshly ground black pepper

Preparation: 5 minutes

Cooking: 5–7 minutes

Serves: 4

Level: 1

TUNA AND ROASTED VEGETABLE SALAD

58

Preheat the oven to 450ºF (230ºC/ gas 8). • Place the onions, bell peppers, and tomatoes in a large roasting pan. Drizzle with 1 tablespoon of oil and the balsamic vinegar. Season with salt and pepper. • Roast for about 20 minutes, until tender. • Arrange the vegetables and olives on a serving plate. Top with the tuna and drizzle with the remaining oil. • Serve warm with the bread.

2   red onions, cut into thick wedges

1   yellow bell pepper (capsicum), halved, seeded, and cut into strips

1   red bell pepper (capsicum), halved, seeded, and cut into strips

1   pound (500 g) cherry tomatoes

2   tablespoons extra-virgin olive oil

1   tablespoon balsamic vinegar

    Salt and freshly ground black pepper

1$\frac{1}{4}$ cups (125 g) black olives

1   (14-ounce/400-g) can tuna in oil, drained

    Ciabatta or other freshly baked bread, to serve

 Preparation: 10 minutes
Cooking: 20 minutes

Serves: 4
Level: 1

FIG, PROSCIUTTO, AND MOZZARELLA SALAD

60

Arrange the arugula and figs on serving plates. • Top with the prosciutto and mozzarella. • Drizzle with the oil and balsamic vinegar. Season with salt and pepper. • Serve.

3   ounces (90 g) arugula (rocket) leaves

8   firm-ripe figs, cut into quarters

12 thin slices prosciutto (Parma ham)

8   small fresh mozzarella balls (bocconcini), drained and sliced

1/4 cup (60 ml) extra-virgin olive oil

1 1/2 tablespoons balsamic vinegar

Salt and freshly ground black pepper

Preparation: 5 minutes

Serves: 4
Level: 1

MUSHROOM, PINE NUT, AND PARMESAN SALAD

Dry-fry the pine nuts in a small frying pan over medium heat until golden, about 3 minutes. • Remove from the heat and set aside. • Add the oil, balsamic vinegar, and mustard to the pan. • Cook over low heat, stirring constantly, until it starts to boil, about 1 minute. • Add the mushrooms and toss until well coated. • Add the pine nuts and chives. Season with salt and pepper. • Arrange the salad greens in a large serving bowl. • Top with the mushrooms and Parmesan and serve.

$^1/_3$ cup (60 g) pine nuts

$^1/_4$ cup (60 ml) extra-virgin olive oil

2 tablespoons balsamic vinegar

1 tablespoon whole-grain mustard

1 pound (500 g) button mushrooms, thinly sliced

2 tablespoons finely chopped chives

Salt and freshly ground black pepper

5 ounces (150 g) baby Asian salad greens

3 ounces (90 g) Parmesan cheese, in shavings

Preparation: 10 minutes
Cooking: 5 minutes

Serves: 4
Level: 1

CHICKEN CAESAR SALAD

To prepare the salad, preheat the broiler (grill). • Place the bread on a baking sheet and drizzle with 1 tablespoon of oil. • Toast about 2 minutes each side, until golden and crisp. • Cook the eggs in a medium saucepan of barely simmering water for 10 minutes. Drain well. Fill the saucepan with cold water and leave the eggs in it for 5 minutes. • Shell the eggs and chop coarsely. • Sauté the bacon in the remaining oil in a large frying pan over medium heat until crisp, about 5 minutes. Set aside to cool a little and until ready to assemble the salad. • Sprinkle the chicken with the seasoning. • Sauté the chicken in the same pan used to cook the bacon until cooked through, about 4 minutes each side. Let cool a little. • Mix the lettuce, cucumber, scallions, bacon, chicken, baguette, and egg in a large salad bowl. Season with salt and pepper.

Salad

1 baguette (French loaf), thinly sliced

2 tablespoons extra-virgin olive oil

2 large eggs

4 slices bacon, coarsely chopped

2 boneless, skinless chicken breasts, thinly sliced

2 teaspoons Cajun seasoning

1 romaine lettuce, torn

1 cucumber, sliced

3 scallions (green onions), thinly sliced

Salt and freshly ground black pepper

Preparation: 10 minutes
Cooking: 20 minutes

Serves: 4
Level: 1

Dressing

1/4 **cup (60 ml) mayonnaise**

2 **tablespoons freshly squeezed lemon juice**

1 **teaspoon Djion mustard**

1 **tablespoon water**

2 **salt-cured anchovy fillets, finely chopped**

4 **tablespoons freshly grated Parmesan**

For the dressing: Mix the mayonnaise, lemon juice, mustard, water, and anchovies in a small bowl. • Drizzle over the salad and toss well. Sprinkle with the Parmesan and serve.

■■■ *Caesar salad is a favorite the world over. It is said to have been invented by Rosa Cardini, the daughter of an Italian immigrant named Cesare Cardini. The Cardinis lived in San Diego, but, during Prohibition, they ran a restaurant just over the border in Tijuana, Mexico. One hot July 4th in 1924, the restaurant was crowded with customers and ingredients were running short. Rosa just used what she had on hand and concocted a salad directly at customers' tables. The salad, which became known as Caesar Salad, became popular, especially with movie stars of the time who were always looking for ways to maintain a trim waistline.*

GARBANZO BEAN AND FETA COUSCOUS SALAD

Put the couscous in a large bowl.
• Pour the boiling water over the couscous. • Cover the bowl with plastic wrap (cling film) and let stand for 10 minutes, until the couscous has completely absorbed the liquid. • Stir in the oil, lemon juice, and zest with a fork.
• Add the scallions, bell pepper, garbanzo beans, feta, olives, parsley, and mint. Season with salt and pepper. • Serve.

Preparation: 20 minutes

Serves: 4
Level: 1

$1^1/2$ cups (300 g)	instant couscous
$1^1/2$ cups (375 ml)	boiling water
2	tablespoons extra-virgin olive oil
2	tablespoons freshly squeezed lemon juice
1	teaspoon finely grated lemon zest
2	scallions (green onions), thinly sliced
1	small yellow bell pepper (capsicum), seeded, and finely chopped
1	(14-ounce/400-g) can garbanzo beans (chick-peas), drained and rinsed
3	ounces (90 g) feta cheese, crumbled
1	cup (100 g) black olives
$1/2$	cup (25 g) finely chopped flat-leaf parsley
1	sprig fresh mint leaves, finely chopped
	Salt and freshly ground black pepper

EGGPLANT AND BUFFALO MOZZARELLA SALAD

Preheat the oven to 450°F (230°C/ gas 8). • Mix the oil and garlic in a small bowl. • Arrange the eggplant slices on a baking sheet. Brush with the oil mixture and season with salt and pepper. • Bake for about 20 minutes, until softened.
• Arrange layers of eggplant, mozzarella, arugula, and tomatoes on individual serving plates. Top with the pesto.
• Serve with crusty bread.

■■■ *The most highly prized mozzarella cheese in Italy is made using buffalo milk. Some cheesemakers in other countries also make buffalo-milk mozzarella. if you can't find it, replace with the same quantity of top quality fresh cows' milk mozzarella.*

1/4 cup (60 ml) extra-virgin olive oil

2 cloves garlic, finely chopped

1 medium eggplant (aubergine), trimmed and cut into 1/2-inch (1-cm) thick slices

Salt and freshly ground black pepper

4 balls fresh buffalo-milk mozzarella cheese, thinly sliced

1 small bunch arugula (rocket)

2 tomatoes, thinly sliced

1/4 cup (60 ml) basil or arugula (rocket) pesto

Crusty bread, to serve

Preparation: 10 minutes

Cooking: 20 minutes

Serves: 4

Level: 1

SHRIMP AND AVOCADO SALAD

To prepare the dill dressing, beat the egg yolk and Dijon mustard in a double boiler over barely simmering water with an electric mixer at high speed until pale. • Gradually beat in the oil in a thin steady trickle until thick. • Add the lemon juice and dill. • Stir in the sour cream and season with salt and pepper. • To prepare the salad, arrange the lettuce, shrimp, and avocado on individual serving plates. • Drizzle with the dill dressing and serve.

Dill Dressing

1   large egg yolk

1   teaspoon Dijon mustard

1/2   cup (125 ml) extra-virgin olive oil

2   teaspoons freshly squeezed lemon juice

2   tablespoons finely chopped fresh dill

1/4   cup (60 ml) sour cream

Salt and freshly ground black pepper

Salad

1   head baby romaine lettuce

24   cooked large shrimp (prawns), peeled and deveined

2   medium ripe avocados, peeled and sliced lengthwise

 Preparation: 25 minutes

Serves: 4

Level: 1

INDIAN RICE SALAD

74

Cook the rice with the turmeric, cardamom pods, and cinnamon stick in a large pan of salted boiling water until tender, 10–15 minutes. • Drain well and transfer to a large bowl. • Dry-fry the mustard seeds in a small frying pan over low heat until aromatic. • Transfer to a small bowl and mix in the oil, white wine vinegar, and sugar. • Add the almonds, golden raisins, garbanzo beans, and cilantro to the rice. • Drizzle with the dressing. • Toss well and serve.

$1^{1}/_{2}$ cups (300 g) basmati rice

$^{1}/_{2}$ teaspoon ground turmeric

2 pods cardamom, lightly crushed

1 stick cinnamon

2 tablespoons mustard seeds

$^{1}/_{4}$ cup (60 ml) grape seed oil

2 tablespoons white wine vinegar

1 tablespoon superfine (caster) sugar

$^{1}/_{3}$ cup (50 g) slivered almonds, roasted

$^{1}/_{3}$ cup (60 g) golden raisins (sultanas)

1 (14-ounce/400-g) can garbanzo beans (chick-peas), drained and rinsed

$^{1}/_{2}$ cup (15 g) coarsely chopped fresh cilantro (coriander)

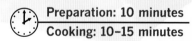

Preparation: 10 minutes
Cooking: 10–15 minutes

Serves: 4
Level: 1

PASTA SALAD WITH TOMATOES, BASIL, AND PARMESAN

Cook the penne in a large pot of salted boiling water until al dente. • Mix the tomatoes, garlic, basil, and oil in a large bowl. Season with salt and pepper. • Preheat the oven to 425°F (220°C/gas 7). • Line a baking sheet with parchment paper. • Sprinkle the cheese onto the sheet. • Bake for 5 minutes until melted and lightly browned. • Remove from the oven and let cool slightly. • Drain the pasta and rinse under cold water to stop the cooking process. Dry well on a clean kitchen towel. • Add the pasta to the bowl with the tomatoes. Mix well and transfer to a serving dish. • Break up the cheese and sprinkle it over the pasta. Garnish with the basil and pine nuts.

1   **pound (500 g) penne pasta**

8   **ounces (250 g) cherry tomatoes, cut into quarters**

4   **cloves garlic, finely chopped**

1   **ounce (30 g) basil leaves, torn**

1/4   **cup (60 ml) extra-virgin olive oil**

  Salt and freshly ground black pepper

1   **cup (125 g) freshly grated Parmesan cheese**

  Sprigs of basil, to garnish

2   **tablespoons pine nuts, toasted**

Preparation: 10 minutes
Cooking: 20 minutes

Serves: 4–6
Level: 1

TUNA, ARTICHOKE, AND WATERCRESS PASTA SALAD

Cook the farfalle in a large pot of salted boiling water until al dente. • Drain the pasta and rinse under cold water to stop the cooking process. Dry well on a clean kitchen towel. Place in a large pasta bowl. • Add the tuna, artichokes, onion, olives, tomatoes, and watercress. • Drizzle with the oil and lemon juice. Season with salt and pepper. • Gently toss to combine.

1	pound (500 g) farfalle pasta
1	(14-ounce/400-g) can tuna in oil, drained and flaked
6	marinated artichoke hearts, drained and thickly sliced
1/2	small red onion, thinly sliced
1/2	cup (50 g) kalamata olives
8	ounces (250 g) cherry tomatoes, halved
2	cups (60 g) watercress sprigs
1/4	cup (60 ml) extra-virgin olive oil
2	tablespoons freshly squeezed lemon juice
	Salt and freshly ground black pepper

■■■ *Farfalle pasta is also known as bow-tie pasta.*
You can also make this pasta salad with penne or another short pasta shape.

Preparation: 15 minutes
Cooking: 12 minutes

Serves: 4
Level: 1

GARBANZO BEAN AND SALMON SALAD

Mix the salmon, garbanzo beans, cucumbers, red onion, and spinach in a large bowl. • Toss well. • Season with salt and pepper. • Mix the yogurt, lemon juice, tahini, and chives in a small bowl. • Spoon the salad onto serving plates and drizzle with the dressing.

1   (8-ounce/250-g) can pink salmon, drained and flaked

1   (14-ounce/400-g) can garbanzo beans (chick-peas), drained and rinsed

2   cucumbers, halved and sliced

1   red onion, thinly sliced

3   cups (100 g) baby spinach leaves

Salt and freshly ground black pepper

1/2 cup (125 ml) plain yogurt

2   tablespoons freshly squeezed lemon juice

1   tablespoon tahini

1   tablespoon finely chopped fresh chives

 Preparation: 15 minutes

Serves: 4
Level: 1

BEAN AND SPINACH SALAD

Mix the cannellini beans, onion, bell pepper, tomatoes, and spinach in a large bowl. • Mix the oil, lemon juice, and sugar in a small bowl. • Drizzle the dressing over the salad and toss well. • Season with salt and pepper. • Spoon into bowls and serve.

1   (14-ounce/400-g) can cannellini beans, drained and rinsed

1   small red onion, thinly sliced

1   red bell pepper (capsicum), seeded and diced

4   tomatoes, cut into wedges

4   ounces (125 g) baby spinach leaves, shredded

2   tablespoons extra-virgin olive oil

2   tablespoons freshly squeezed lemon juice

1/8 teaspoon sugar

Salt and freshly ground black pepper

Preparation: 10 minutes

Serves: 4
Level: 1

SOUPS

THAI TOFU AND MUSHROOM SOUP

Sauté the mushrooms in the oil in a large saucepan over medium heat until softened, about 3 minutes. • Add the curry paste and cook for 1 minute while stirring until aromatic. • Stir in the vegetable stock, coconut milk, fish sauce, lime juice, tofu, and scallions. Bring to a boil. • Cover and simmer over medium-low heat for 5 minutes. • Ladle the soup into bowls. Garnish with the cilantro and serve hot.

8	ounces (250 g) button mushrooms, thinly sliced
1/4	cup (60 ml) peanut oil
1/3	cup (90 ml) Thai red curry paste
4	cups (1 liter) vegetable stock
2	cups (500 ml) coconut milk
1	tablespoon Asian fish sauce
1	tablespoon freshly squeezed lime juice
8	ounces (250 g) firm tofu, cut into small cubes
3	scallions (green onions), thinly sliced
1	bunch fresh cilantro (coriander) leaves

Preparation: 10 minutes

Cooking: 10 minutes

Serves: 4
Level: 1

■■■ Red curry paste is a Thai condiment used to flavor soups, curries, and stir-fries. You can buy it at Asian food stores or online.

CREAMY MUSHROOM SOUP WITH THYME

88

Sauté the onion, garlic, and mushrooms in the oil in a large saucepan over medium heat until softened, about 3 minutes. • Pour in the stock and cream. Bring to a boil. • Cover and simmer over low heat for 5 minutes. • Pour the mixture into a food processor and process until smooth. • Stir in the thyme and season with salt and pepper. • Ladle the soup into bowls. • Garnish with the thyme leaves and serve hot.

1	onion, finely chopped
2	cloves garlic, finely chopped
1	pound (500 g) white mushrooms, coarsely chopped
2	tablespoons extra-virgin olive oil
4	cups (1 liter) vegetable stock
1	cup (250 ml) light (single) cream
2	tablespoons fresh thyme leaves, + extra leaves to garnish
	Salt and freshly ground black pepper

Preparation: 10 minutes
Cooking: 10 minutes

Serves: 4
Level: 1

■ ■ ■ *The fresh thyme sets off the flavors of the mushrooms beautifully in this creamy soup. For the best flavor, use homemade vegetable stock. Although making stock takes time, remember that it can be made ahead of time and frozen for future use.*

CHICKEN AND CORN SOUP

Sauté the garlic and ginger in the oil in a large saucepan over medium-low heat until aromatic, about 1 minute. • Pour in the chicken stock and creamed corn. Add the chicken and soy sauce. Bring to a boil. • Simmer over medium heat for 5 minutes. • Mix the cornstarch and cold water in a small bowl until smooth. • Add the cornstarch mixture to the soup and stir until it starts to thicken, about 30 seconds. • Gradually pour in the egg, stirring constantly. Cook for about 1 minute, until the egg is cooked. • Ladle the soup into bowls. • Garnish with the scallions and serve hot.

2   cloves garlic, finely chopped

2   teaspoons grated fresh ginger

2   teaspoons peanut oil

2^1/$_2$ cups (625 ml) chicken stock

2^1/$_2$ cups (625 ml) canned creamed corn (sweet corn)

2   cups (200 g) shredded cooked chicken

1   tablespoon light soy sauce

2   teaspoons cornstarch (cornflour)

2   tablespoons cold water

1   large egg, lightly beaten

2   scallions (green onions), thinly sliced

Preparation: 10 minutes
Cooking: 8 minutes

Serves: 4
Level: 1

TOMATO, VEGETABLE, AND BEAN SOUP

Sauté the onion and garlic in the oil in a large saucepan over medium-low heat until softened, about 3 minutes. • Add the vegetable stock, tomatoes, tomato paste, zucchini, carrot, and celery. Bring to a boil. • Cover and simmer over medium-low heat until the zucchini are tender, about 15 minutes. • Add the borlotti beans and basil. Season with salt and pepper. • Simmer for 2 minutes. • Ladle the soup into bowls and serve hot.

1   onion, finely chopped

2   cloves garlic, finely chopped

1   tablespoon extra-virgin olive oil

4   cups (1 liter) vegetable stock

2   pounds (1 kg) tomatoes, chopped

2   tablespoons tomato paste

2   zucchini (courgettes), halved lengthwise and thinly sliced

1   large carrot, finely chopped

2   stalks celery, thinly sliced

1   (14-ounce/400-g) can borlotti or red kidney beans, drained and rinsed

1   small sprig basil leaves

Salt and freshly ground black pepper

Preparation: 10 minutes
Cooking: 20 minutes

Serves: 4
Level: 1

SPICY PUMPKIN SOUP

Sauté the onion and garlic in the oil in a large saucepan over medium-low heat until softened, about 3 minutes. • Add the Cajun spices and cook, stirring, for 1 minute. • Add the pumpkin, stirring well to coat it with the Cajun spices. • Pour in the vegetable stock and bring to a boil. • Cover and simmer over low heat until the pumpkin is tender, 15–20 minutes. • Pour the mixture into a food processor and process until smooth. • Season with salt and pepper. • Ladle the soup into bowls. Garnish with the chives and serve hot.

1	onion, finely chopped
2	cloves garlic, finely chopped
1	tablespoon extra-virgin olive oil
2	teaspoons Cajun spices
2	pounds (1 kg) pumpkin or winter squash, cut into small cubes
5	cups (1.25 liters) vegetable stock
	Salt and freshly ground black pepper
1	tablespoon finely chopped fresh chives

Preparation: 10 minutes
Cooking: 20 minutes

Serves: 4
Level: 1

■ ■ ■ *If preferred, replace the prosciutto in this salad with eight large slices of salami.*

LEEK AND POTATO SOUP

Sauté the leeks and garlic in the oil in a large saucepan over medium-low heat until softened, about 3 minutes. • Pour in the chicken stock. Add the potatoes and rosemary. Bring to a boil. • Cover and simmer over low heat until the potatoes are tender, about 15 minutes. • Stir in the lemon juice and season with salt and pepper. • Ladle the soup into bowls and serve hot.

2	leeks, thinly sliced
2	cloves garlic, finely chopped
1	tablespoon extra-virgin olive oil
5	cups (1.25 liters) chicken stock
2	pounds (1 kg) potatoes, peeled and cut into small cubes
1	tablespoon finely chopped fresh rosemary
2	tablespoons freshly squeezed lemon juice
	Salt and freshly ground black pepper

Preparation: 10 minutes
Cooking: 20 minutes

Serves: 4
Level: 1

TOMATO AND LENTIL SOUP

Sauté the onion and garlic in the oil in a large saucepan over medium-low heat until softened, about 3 minutes. • Add the curry paste and cook, stirring, for 1 minute. • Pour in the vegetable stock, tomatoes, and lentils. Bring to a boil. • Cover and simmer over low heat, stirring from time to time, until the lentils are tender, about 20 minutes. • Season with salt and pepper. • Ladle the soup into bowls and serve hot.

1   onion, finely chopped

2   cloves garlic, finely chopped

2   tablespoons extra-virgin olive oil

2   tablespoons mild curry paste

4   cups (1 liter) vegetable stock

2   (14-ounce/400-g) can tomatoes, with juice

1   cup (100 g) red lentils

    Salt and freshly ground black pepper

Preparation: 10 minutes
Cooking: 24 minutes

Serves: 4
Level: 1

MINTED PEA SOUP

Sauté the onion and garlic in the oil in a large saucepan over medium-low heat until softened, about 3 minutes. • Pour in the stock. Bring to a boil. • Add the peas and mint, reserving a little for a garnish. • Cover and simmer over low heat for 5 minutes. • Pour the mixture into a food processor and process until smooth. • Return the soup to the saucepan. Stir in the sour cream. Season with salt and pepper. • Simmer over low heat for 5 minutes. • Ladle the soup into bowls, garnish with the reserved mint, and serve hot.

1   onion, finely chopped

2   cloves garlic, finely chopped

2   tablespoons extra-virgin olive oil

$2^{1}/_{2}$ cups (625 ml) chicken stock

2   pounds (1 kg) frozen peas, thawed

1   small bunch fresh mint, coarsely chopped

$^{1}/_{3}$ cup (90 ml) sour cream

   Salt and freshly ground black pepper

Preparation: 10 minutes

Cooking: 15 minutes

Serves: 4

Level: 1

HOT AND SOUR CHICKEN SOUP

Bring the chicken stock to a boil in a large saucepan over high heat. • Add the garlic, lemon grass, 1 chile pepper, and half the kaffir lime leaves. Bring to a boil. • Strain the stock into a large bowl. • Return the stock to the saucepan. • Cover and simmer over medium-low heat for 10 minutes. • Add the lime juice, fish sauce, jaggery, and remaining chile pepper to the soup. • Stir in half the cilantro. • Divide the shredded chicken among the serving bowls. • Ladle the soup over the chicken. • Garnish with the remaining kaffir lime leaves and cilantro and serve hot.

6 cups (1.5 liters) chicken stock

2 cloves garlic, finely chopped

2 stems lemon grass, coarsely chopped

2 small red Thai chiles, seeded and finely sliced

6 kaffir lime leaves, finely shredded

2 tablespoons freshly squeezed lime juice

2 tablespoons Asian fish sauce

2 teaspoons jaggery (palm sugar) or brown sugar

1/2 cup (25 g) cilantro (coriander) leaves

2 cups (200 g) shredded cooked chicken

Preparation: 10 minutes
Cooking: 15 minutes

Serves: 4–6
Level: 1

■■■ *Kaffir lime, also known as makrut lime, is a member of the citrus family. The fruit is knobbly and bitter-tasting, and it is the leaves that are most commonly used to flavor food. If you can't find the lime leaves for this dish, it is okay to leave them out.*

SPICED CAULIFLOWER SOUP

Sauté the onion and garlic in the oil in a large saucepan over medium-low heat until softened, about 3 minutes. • Stir in the turmeric, coriander, and cumin and cook for 1 minute. • Add the cauliflower and potato. Pour in the stock. Bring to a boil. • Cover and simmer over low heat until the cauliflower and potato are tender, 10–12 minutes. • Pour the mixture into a food processor and process until smooth. • Stir in the yogurt and season with salt and pepper. • Ladle the soup into bowls. • Garnish with the parsley and serve hot with the toast.

1   **onion, finely chopped**

2   **cloves garlic, finely chopped**

2   **tablespoons vegetable oil**

1   **teaspoon ground turmeric**

1   **teaspoon ground coriander**

1   **teaspoon ground cumin**

$1^1/_2$ **pounds (750 g) cauliflower, cut into florets**

1   **potato, peeled and cut into cubes**

4   **cups (1 liter) chicken or vegetable stock**

$^1/_3$ **cup (90 ml) plain yogurt**

Salt and freshly ground black pepper

Sprigs of parsley, to garnish

Toast, to serve

Preparation: **10 minutes**

Cooking: **15–17 minutes**

Serves: **4**

Level: **1**

CREAMY TOMATO SOUP

Sauté the onion and garlic in the oil in a large saucepan over medium-low heat until softened, about 3 minutes. • Add the tomatoes, stock, bay leaves, and sugar. • Break the tomatoes up using a wooden spoon. • Bring to a boil. • Cover and simmer over low heat for 10 minutes. • Discard the bay leaves. • Pour the mixture into a food processor and process until smooth. • Return the soup to the saucepan. Stir in the cream. Season with salt and pepper. • Simmer over low heat for 5 minutes. • Ladle the soup into bowls. • Garnish with the basil and serve hot.

1   onion, finely chopped

3   cloves garlic, finely chopped

2   tablespoons extra-virgin olive oil

2   (14-ounce/400-g) cans tomatoes, with juice

$1^1/_2$ cups (375 ml) vegetable or chicken stock

2   bay leaves

1   teaspoon sugar

$^1/_2$ cup (125 ml) light (single) cream

Salt and freshly ground black pepper

Sprigs of basil, to garnish

Preparation: 10 minutes
Cooking: 20 minutes

Serves: 4
Level: 1

CREAMY TOMATO SOUP WITH SOUR CREAM

108

Sauté the onions and thyme in the oil in a large saucepan over medium-low heat until softened, about 3 minutes. • Stir in the tomatoes and season with salt and pepper. • Cook for 2 minutes. • Pour in the water and bring to a boil. • Simmer over medium heat for 10 minutes. • Discard the thyme. • Pour the mixture into a food processor and process until smooth. • Return the soup to the saucepan. Stir in the cream. • Simmer over low heat for 5 minutes. • Ladle the soup into bowls. • Garnish with the sour cream and cilantro. Serve hot.

2 large onions, finely chopped

1 sprig thyme

1/4 cup (60 ml) extra-virgin olive oil

4 pounds (2 kg) ripe tomatoes, peeled and coarsely chopped

Salt and freshly ground black pepper

Generous 3/4 cup (200 ml) boiling water

3/4 cup (180 ml) heavy (double) cream

2/3 cup (150 g) sour cream

Sprigs of cilantro (coriander), to garnish

Preparation: 10 minutes
Cooking: 20 minutes

Serves: 6–8
Level: 1

CHORIZO, BEAN, AND SPINACH SOUP

Sauté the chorizo and onion in the oil in a large saucepan over medium-high heat until the onion is softened, about 5 minutes. • Add the garlic and tomato paste. • Sauté for 1 minute. • Pour in the chicken stock, tomatoes, and beans. Bring to a boil. • Simmer over medium heat for 10 minutes. • Stir in the spinach and season with salt and pepper. • Cook until the spinach has wilted, about 3 minutes. • Ladle the soup into bowls and serve hot.

12 ounces (350 g) dried Spanish chorizo sausage, diced

1 onion, finely chopped

1 tablespoon extra-virgin olive oil

2 cloves garlic, finely chopped

2 tablespoons tomato paste

5 cups (1.25 liters) chicken stock

1 (14-ounce/400 g) can tomatoes, with juice

1 (14-ounce/400 g) can cannellini beans, drained and rinsed

4 ounces (125 g) baby spinach leaves

Salt and freshly ground black pepper

Preparation: 5 minutes
Cooking: 20 minutes

Serves: 4
Level: 1

GAZPACHO

Combine the tomatoes, bell pepper, cucumber, scallion, bread crumbs, almonds, and garlic in a food processor and process until smooth. • Add the oil, vinegar, and water. Season with salt and pepper. • Process for a few seconds more until well mixed. • Ladle the soup into serving bowls. • Garnish with the remaining thinly sliced bell pepper and cilantro. • Serve at once.

■■■ *Make sure all the ingredients for this cool soup are well chilled in the refrigerator. Take them out just before you make the soup and keep it well chilled until you serve it.*

1	pound (500 g) firm-ripe tomatoes, peeled
1	red bell pepper (capsicum), seeded, cored, and coarsely chopped, + extra to garnish
1	cucumber, peeled and finely chopped
1	scallion (spring onion), finely chopped
4	cups (250 g) fresh bread crumbs
1/2	cup (75 g) almonds, toasted
1	clove garlic, peeled
1/4	cup (60 ml) extra-virgin olive oil
2	tablespoons white wine vinegar
4	cups (1 liter) ice-cold water
	Salt and freshly ground black pepper
	Fresh cilantro (coriander) leaves, to garnish

 Preparation: 5 minutes

Serves: 4
Level: 1

PASTA

SPAGHETTI WITH PEAS, CRISP BACON, AND PARMESAN

Cook the spaghetti in a large saucepan of salted boiling water, until al dente, about 10 minutes • Meanwhile, heat the oil in a large frying pan over medium-high heat. • Sauté the bacon and onion, until the bacon is crisp, about 5 minutes. Remove from the pan and keep warm. • Add the chicken stock to the pan and bring to a boil. • Add the peas and mint. Cover and simmer until the peas are tender, about 2 minutes. • Drain the pasta and return to the pan. • Add the pea mixture, bacon and onion mixture, and Parmesan. • Season with salt and pepper. Toss over low heat until well combined. Serve hot.

1	pound (500 g) spaghetti
1	tablespoon extra-virgin olive oil
6	ounces (180 g) bacon slices, coarsely chopped
1	onion, finely chopped
1/2	cup (125 ml) chicken stock
1	cup (150 g) frozen peas
2	tablespoons finely chopped fresh mint
5	ounces (150 g) Parmesan cheese, shaved
	Salt and freshly ground black pepper

Preparation: 10 minutes
Cooking: 15 minutes

Serves: 4
Level: 1

BUCATINI WITH GARLIC, TUNA, AND CHERRY TOMATOES

Cook the bucatini in a large saucepan of salted boiling water until al dente, 10–12 minutes. • Drain and keep warm. • Heat the oil in a saucepan over high heat. • Sauté the tomatoes, garlic, and sugar until the tomatoes are just soft, about 5 minutes. • Stir in oregano and season with salt and pepper. • Add the bucatini and tuna to the tomato mixture. • Toss over low heat until well combined. Serve hot.

1   pound (500 g) bucatini or spaghetti

3   tablespoons extra-virgin olive oil

1   pound (500 g) cherry tomatoes, halved

3   cloves garlic, finely chopped

$1/2$ teaspoon sugar

2   tablespoons fresh oregano leaves

Salt and freshly ground black pepper

1   (14-ounce/400-g) can tuna in oil, drained and flaked

Preparation: 5 minutes

Cooking: 15 minutes

Serves: 4
Level: 1

SPAGHETTI WITH CHERRY TOMATOES

Cook the spaghetti in a large pot of salted, boiling water until al dente, 10–12 minutes. • Mix the oil, oregano, chile pepper, and garlic in a small bowl. • Heat a large frying pan over medium heat. Add the oil mixture and sauté until the garlic is pale gold, about 2 minutes. • Add the tomatoes and sauté for 3 minutes. • Drain the pasta and add to the tomatoes. Season with salt. Add the mozzarella and toss well. • Serve hot.

1	pound (500 g) spaghetti
$1/3$	cup (90 ml) extra-virgin olive oil
1	tablespoons finely chopped fresh oregano
1	dried red chile, finely chopped
2	cloves garlic, lightly crushed but left whole
2	pounds (1 kg) cherry tomatoes, halved
	Salt
8	ounces (250 g) small mozzarella balls (bocconcini), halved

Preparation: 10 minutes
Cooking: 10–15 minutes

Serves: 4–6
Level: 1

SPAGHETTI WITH SPICY TUNA AND THYME

Toss the tuna in the flour, shaking to remove the excess. • Heat the oil in a large frying pan over medium heat. Add the garlic, olives, chiles, and 1 tablespoon of thyme. Sauté for 2 minutes. • Season with salt and pepper. Add the tuna and zucchini. Cook over medium heat until the fish is cooked through, 5–6 minutes. • Drizzle with the wine and let it evaporate for 2 minutes. • Meanwhile, cook the pasta in a large pot of salted, boiling water until al dente, 10–12 minutes. • Drain and add to the tuna. Toss well. Sprinkle with the extra thyme. • Serve hot.

1	pound (500 g) tuna steak, cut into small pieces
2	tablespoons all-purpose (plain) flour
1/4	cup (60 ml) extra-virgin olive oil
1	clove garlic, finely chopped
20	black olives, pitted and finely chopped
2	fresh red or green chiles, seeded and finely chopped
1	tablespoon finely chopped fresh thyme or parsley + extra, to garnish
	Salt and freshly ground black pepper
4	medium zucchini (courgettes), diced
1/2	cup (125 ml) dry white wine
1	pound (500 g) spaghetti

Preparation: 10 minutes
Cooking: 20 minutes

Serves: 4
Level: 1

SPAGHETTI WITH CLAMS

Place 1 clove of garlic and half the parsley in 2 tablespoons of oil in a large saucepan. Add the clams and cook over high heat until open, 5–10 minutes. Discard any clams that do not open.
• Cook the remaining garlic, chile pepper, and chopped tomatoes in a large saucepan over medium heat for 10 minutes. • Season with salt and pepper. Add the clams and their cooking liquid.
• Meanwhile, cook the pasta in a large pot of salted, boiling water until al dente, 10–12 minutes. • Drain and add to the clam sauce. Season generously with pepper and add the remaining parsley. Toss well. • Serve hot.

3	cloves garlic, finely chopped
2	tablespoons finely chopped fresh parsley
1/3	cup (90 ml) extra-virgin olive oil
2	pounds (1 kg) clams, in shell
1	fresh red chile, seeded and finely chopped
1	pound (500 g) ripe tomatoes, peeled and chopped
	Salt and freshly ground black pepper
1	pound (500 g) spaghetti

 Preparation: 15 minutes
Cooking: 15 minutes

Serves: 4–6
Level: 2

PENNE WITH ASPARAGUS, MUSHROOMS, AND CHILE

Cook the pasta in a large saucepan of salted boiling water until al dente, about 10 minutes. • Drain and set aside. • Heat the oil in a large frying pan over medium heat. • Sauté the garlic, chiles, mushrooms, and asparagus until soft, about 3 minutes. • Return the pasta to the pan. • Stir in the stock, spinach, thyme, and mushroom mixture. Season with salt and pepper. • Stir until heated through, about 2 minutes. Serve hot.

1	pound (500 g) penne
3	tablespoons extra-virgin olive oil
2	cloves garlic, crushed
2	small fresh red chiles, seeds removed and finely chopped
8	ounces (250 g) button mushrooms, sliced
1	bunch asparagus, cut into short lengths
1	cup (250 ml) chicken stock
3	ounces (90 g) baby spinach leaves
2	tablespoons fresh thyme leaves
	Salt and freshly ground black pepper

Preparation: 10 minutes
Cooking: 10 minutes

Serves: 4
Level: 1

FETTUCCINE WITH SALMON AND CAPERS

Cook the pasta in a large saucepan of salted boiling water until al dente, about 3–5 minutes. • Drain and place in a large heated bowl. • Meanwhile, heat the oil in a large saucepan over medium heat. • Sauté the salmon until nearly cooked, about 3 minutes each side. Stir in the lemon juice. • Transfer the salmon to a plate and flake. • Add the scallions, cream, capers, salmon, and parsley to the pasta in the bowl. • Season with salt and pepper. Toss thoroughly and serve hot.

1	pound (500 g) fettuccine
3	tablespoons extra-virgin olive oil
14	ounces (400 g) salmon fillet
1/3	cup (90 ml) freshly squeezed lemon juice
4	scallions (green onions), thinly sliced
1 1/2	cups (375 ml) light (single) cream
1 1/2	tablespoons capers
2	tablespoons finely chopped fresh flat-leaf parsley
	Salt and freshly ground black pepper

Preparation: 10 minutes

Cooking: 3–5 minutes

Serves: 4
Level: 1

FETTUCCINE WITH CHICKEN, CREAM, AND CHIVES

Cook the fettuccine in a large saucepan of salted boiling water, until al dente, 3–5 minutes. • Meanwhile, heat the oil in a large frying pan over medium-high heat. • Sauté the garlic and leek until tender, about 5 minutes. • Add the wine and simmer for 1 minute. • Add the cream, chives, and chicken. • Season with salt and pepper. • Cover and simmer over medium heat until warmed through, 3–5 minutes. • Drain the fettuccine and return to pan. • Add the cream sauce. • Toss over low heat until well combined. Serve hot.

1	pound (500 g) fettuccine
3	tablespoons extra-virgin olive oil
2	cloves garlic, crushed
1	leek, trimmed, halved lengthwise, and thinly sliced
$^1/_2$	cup (125 ml) dry white wine
$1^1/_2$	cups (375 ml) light (single) cream
2	tablespoons finely chopped fresh chives
2	cups (300 g) cooked shredded chicken
	Salt and freshly ground black pepper

Preparation: 15 minutes
Cooking: 10 minutes

Serves: 4
Level: 1

PEPPERED MUSHROOM MACARONI

Cook the macaroni in a large saucepan of salted boiling water until al dente, about 10 minutes. • Meanwhile, heat the butter and oil in a large frying pan over medium-high heat. • Sauté the mushrooms and scallions until tender, 4–5 minutes. • Season with salt and stir in the cracked pepper. • Stir in the cream and cook until heated through, about 3 minutes. • Drain the macaroni and return to the pan. • Add the mushroom mixture, parsley, and cheese. • Toss over low heat until the cheese melts. Serve hot.

1	pound (500 g) macaroni
2	tablespoons butter
3	tablespoons extra-virgin olive oil
10	ounces (300 g) button mushrooms, thinly sliced
4	scallions (green onions), thinly sliced
	Salt
1	teaspoon cracked black pepper
1	cup (250 ml) heavy (double) cream
2	tablespoons coarsely chopped fresh flat-leaf parsley
8	ounces (250 g) freshly grated mozzarella cheese

Preparation: 10 minutes
Cooking: 15 minutes

Serves: 4
Level: 1

THREE-CHEESE PENNE

Cook the penne in a large saucepan of salted boiling water until al dente, 10–12 minutes. • Drain the penne and return to the pan. • Add the cheeses, cream, and chives. • Toss gently to combine. • Season with salt and pepper. • Spoon into four 2-cup (500-ml) greased shallow ovenproof dishes. • Preheat a broiler (grill) on high heat. • Place the dishes under the broiler and cook until hot and bubbling, 3–5 minutes. • Sprinkle with the basil leaves and serve hot.

1	pound (500 g) penne
5	ounces (150 g) Gruyère cheese, freshly grated
3	ounces (90 g) cheddar cheese, freshly grated
5	ounces (150 g) goat cheese, crumbled
1/2	cup (125 ml) light (single) cream
2	tablespoons chopped chives
	Salt and freshly ground black pepper
1/2	cup basil leaves, to serve

Preparation: 10 minutes
Cooking: 20 minutes

Serves: 4
Level: 1

PASTA ALLA PUTTANESCA

Cook the pasta in a large saucepan of salted boiling water until al dente, 10–12 minutes. • Heat the oil in a large frying pan over medium heat. Sauté the garlic, chile, and tomatoes until tender, about 5 minutes. • Stir in the olives, anchovies, and capers. • Simmer, stirring from time to time, until boiling, about 5 minutes. • Drain the pasta and return to the pan. • Add the tomato mixture and the basil. Season with salt and pepper. • Toss over low heat until well combined. Serve hot.

1	pound (500 g) tortiglioni or rigatoni
1/4	cup (60 ml) extra-virgin olive oil
2	cloves garlic, finely chopped
1	long red fresh chile, seeded and finely sliced
6	ripe tomatoes, seeded and coarsely chopped
1/2	cup (75 g) black olives
4	anchovy fillets, drained and coarsely chopped
2	tablespoons salt-cured capers, rinsed
1	cup (30 g) small basil leaves
	Salt and freshly ground black pepper

Preparation: 15 minutes

Cooking: 12 minutes

Serves: 4

Level: 1

TOMATO, ARUGULA, AND BLACK OLIVE LINGUINE

138

Cook the linguine in a large saucepan of salted boiling water until al dente, 10–12 minutes. • Meanwhile, combine the tomato sauce, sugar, and bay leaves in a saucepan. • Cover and simmer over low heat, stirring from time to time, for 10 minutes. • Season with salt and pepper. • Remove the bay leaves. • Drain the linguine and return to the pan. • Add the tomato sauce, olives, and arugula. • Toss until well combined. Serve hot.

1 pound (500 g) linguine

2 cups (500 ml) tomato pasta sauce

1 teaspoon sugar

2 bay leaves

Salt and freshly ground black pepper

1/2 cup (90 g) small black olives

3 ounces (90 g) baby arugula (rocket) leaves

Preparation: 10 minutes
Cooking: 12 minutes

Serves: 4
Level: 1

FARFALLE WITH BEANS AND PESTO

To prepare the pasta: Bring a large pot of salted water to a boil. Add the green beans and return to a boil. • Add the pasta and cook for 5 minutes. • Add the peas and cook until the pasta is al dente. • To make the pesto: Chop the basil, pine nuts, garlic, oil, and salt in a food processor until smooth. Stir in the cheese. • Drain the pasta and vegetables and toss gently with the pesto. Stir in the kidney beans and walnuts. Drizzle with the oil and garnish with the basil leaves. • Serve hot.

Pasta

5 ounces (150 g) green beans, cut into short lengths

1 pound (500 g) farfalle

1 cup (150 g) fresh or frozen peas

1 cup (200 g) canned red kidney beans, drained and rinsed

1/2 cup (50 g) chopped walnuts

1/4 cup (60 ml) extra-virgin olive oil

Basil leaves, to garnish

Pesto

1 large bunch fresh basil

2 tablespoons pine nuts

2 cloves garlic

1/2 cup (125 ml) extra-virgin olive oil

Salt

4 tablespoons freshly grated Parmesan cheese

Preparation: 10 minutes

Cooking: 15 minutes

Serves: 4–6
Level: 1

TAGLIATELLE WITH WALNUT SAUCE

Blanch the walnuts in boiling water for 1 minute. Drain and transfer to a cloth. Roll the nuts firmly under your fingers to remove the skins. • Put the walnuts, garlic, and bread crumbs in the bowl of a food processor and process until finely chopped. • Add the cream, Parmesan, oil, and cinnamon and process until smooth. Season with salt and pepper.
• Cook the pasta in a large pot of salted, boiling water until al dente, 3–5 minutes.
• Drain and transfer to a large bowl. Add the walnut sauce and toss gently. Garnish with walnut halves and serve hot.

1	cup (125 g) walnuts + extra walnut halves, to garnish
1	clove garlic, peeled
1	cup (60 g) fresh bread crumbs
3/4	cup (180 ml) heavy (double) cream
1/2	cup (60 g) freshly grated Parmesan cheese
3	tablespoons extra-virgin olive oil
1/4	teaspoon ground cinnamon
	Salt and freshly ground black pepper
1	pound (500 g) fresh tagliatelle or fettuccine

Preparation: 20 minutes
Cooking: 4–6 minutes

Serves: 4
Level: 2

TAGLIATELLE WITH VEGETABLE SAUCE

Sauté the onion and garlic in half the oil in a large frying pan over medium heat until softened. • Add the zucchini, bell pepper, carrot, and basil. Sauté for 2–3 minutes. • Stir in the tomatoes. Cover and simmer for 10 minutes until all the vegetables are tender. • Discard the garlic. Season with salt and pepper. • Meanwhile, cook the pasta in a large pot of salted, boiling water until al dente, 3–5 minutes. • Drain and add to the sauce. Toss over medium heat for 1 minute. • Sprinkle with the parsley and drizzle with the remaining oil. Garnish with the extra basil and serve hot.

1	onion, finely chopped
2	cloves garlic, lightly crushed but left whole
1/3	cup (90 ml) extra-virgin olive oil
2	zucchini (courgettes), very thinly sliced
1	red bell pepper (capsicum), seeded and thinly sliced
1	large carrot, very thinly sliced
2	sprigs basil, torn + extra, to garnish
1	pound (500 g) tomatoes, peeled and chopped
	Salt and freshly ground black pepper
1	pound (500 g) fresh tagliatelle or fettuccine
1	tablespoon finely chopped fresh parsley

Preparation: 15 minutes
Cooking: 15 minutes

Serves: 4
Level: 1

GRAINS

ROAST PUMPKIN AND ARUGULA RISOTTO

Preheat the oven to 450°F (230°C/gas 8). • Place the pumpkin in a roasting pan. Drizzle with 1 tablespoon of oil.
• Bake for 20 minutes, until tender.
• Meanwhile, sauté the onion and garlic in the remaining oil in a large, deep frying pan over medium heat until softened, about 3 minutes. • Add the rice and cook for 2 minutes, stirring constantly. • Gradually add the stock, 1/2 cup (125 ml) at a time. Cook and stir until each addition has been absorbed.
• Add the roasted pumpkin and arugula with the last 1/2 cup of stock. • Cook and stir until the rice is tender. The whole process should take 15–18 minutes.
• Season with pepper. • Sprinkle with the Parmesan and serve hot.

1 pound (500 g) pumpkin or winter squash, peeled and cut into 1/2-inch (1-cm) cubes

2 tablespoons extra-virgin olive oil

1 onion, finely chopped

2 cloves garlic, finely chopped

2 cups (400 g) Italian risotto rice (Arborio, Carnaroli, or Vialone Nano)

4 cups (1 liter) vegetable stock, boiling

5 ounces (150 g) arugula (rocket), finely shredded

Freshly ground black pepper

1/2 cup (60 g) freshly grated Parmesan cheese

Preparation: 10 minutes
Cooking: 20 minutes

Serves: 4
Level: 1

CHAMPAGNE AND CILANTRO RISOTTO

Sauté the onion in 2 tablespoons of butter in a large, deep frying pan over medium heat until softened, about 3 minutes. • Add the rice and cook for 2 minutes, stirring constantly. • Pour in the Champagne and cook over high heat for 3 minutes. • Gradually add the stock, 1/2 cup (125 ml) at a time. Cook and stir until each addition has been absorbed and the rice is tender, 15–18 minutes. • Season with salt and pepper. Stir in the remaining butter. • Sprinkle with the cilantro and Parmesan. • Serve hot.

1 large onion, finely chopped

1/4 cup (60 g) butter

2 cups (400 g) Italian risotto rice (Arborio, Carnaroli, or Vialone Nano)

3/4 cup (180 ml) Champagne or dry sparkling white wine

3 cups (750 ml) vegetable stock, boiling

Salt and freshly ground black pepper

2 tablespoons finely chopped fresh cilantro (coriander)

3 ounces (90 g) Parmesan cheese, cut into shavings

Preparation: 5 minutes
Cooking: 20 minutes

Serves: 4
Level: 1

VEGETABLE RISOTTO WITH SMOKED CHEESE

Sauté the shallots in 2 tablespoons of the butter and oil in a large, deep frying pan over medium heat for about 3 minutes, until softened. • Add the rice and cook for 2 minutes, stirring constantly. • Pour in the wine and cook over high heat for 3 minutes. • Stir in the mixed vegetables. • Gradually add the stock, 1/2 cup (125 ml) at a time. Cook and stir until each addition has been absorbed and the rice is tender, 15–18 minutes. • Remove from the heat and stir in the cubes of provolone, the remaining butter, and parsley. Season with salt and pepper. Arrange the sliced provolone on top of the risotto and serve hot.

2   shallots,
    finely chopped

1/3 cup (90 g) butter

2   tablespoons extra-
    virgin olive oil

2   cups (400 g) Italian
    risotto rice (Arborio,
    Carnaroli, or Vialone
    Nano)

1/3 cup (90 ml)
    dry white wine

2   cups (300 g) mixed
    frozen vegetables

4   cups (1 liter)
    vegetable stock,
    boiling

3   ounces (90 g)
    smoked provolone
    or other mild
    smoked cheese,
    cubed

1   tablespoon finely
    chopped parsley

    Salt and freshly
    ground black pepper

2   ounces (60 g)
    smoked provolone
    or other mild
    smoked cheese,
    thinly sliced

Preparation: 10 minutes
Cooking: 20 minutes

Serves: 4
Level: 1

CREAMY TROUT RISOTTO WITH CAPERS

154

Sauté the leek and garlic in 1 tablespoon of oil in a large, deep frying pan over medium-low heat until softened, about 3 minutes. • Add the rice and cook for 2 minutes, stirring constantly. • Gradually add the stock, $1/2$ cup (125 ml) at a time. Cook and stir until each addition has been absorbed. • Meanwhile, sauté the trout in the remaining oil in a large frying pan over medium heat for 3 minutes. • Transfer to a plate and break the trout into flakes using a fork. • Add the trout and capers with the last $1/2$ cup of stock. • Cook and stir until the rice is tender. The whole process should take 15–18 minutes. • Stir in the cream and dill. Season with pepper. • Let stand for 5 minutes. • Serve hot.

1	leek, thinly sliced
2	cloves garlic, finely chopped
2	tablespoons extra-virgin olive oil
2	cups (400 g) Italian risotto rice (Arborio, Carnaroli, or Vialone Nano)
4	cups (1 liter) fish or vegetable stock, boiling
10	ounces (300 g) trout fillets
2	tablespoons salt-cured capers, rinsed
1	cup (250 ml) light (single) cream
2	tablespoons finely chopped fresh dill
	Freshly ground black pepper

Preparation: 10 minutes
Cooking: 20 minutes

Serves: 4
Level: 1

SEAFOOD PAELLA

Preheat the oven to 400°F (200°C/ gas 6). • Sauté the onion, garlic, and bell pepper in the oil in a paella pan or large frying pan over medium heat until softened, about 3 minutes. • Stir in the rice, mixed seafood, peas, and saffron. • Pour in the fish stock and bring to a boil. Season with salt and pepper. • Cook over medium-high heat until all the liquid has almost been absorbed, about 10 minutes. The rice grains should still be slightly crunchy, and there should still be liquid in the pan. • Bake in the oven, uncovered, for 10 minutes. • Add the parsley, garnish with the lemon wedges, and serve hot.

■■■ *Paella is a classic Spanish dish. If possible, use short-grain Spanish rice, which absorbs liquid well and stays relatively firm during cooking. The rice should be dry and separate when done, not creamy like risotto.*

1   onion, finely chopped

2   cloves garlic, finely chopped

1   small red bell pepper (capsicum), seeded and cut into small cubes

1   tablespoon extra-virgin olive oil

2   cups (400 g) short-grain rice

1³/₄ pounds (750 g) fresh mixed seafood (mussels, clams, shrimp. etc.), cleaned

³/₄ cup (90 g) frozen peas, thawed

¹/₂ teaspoon saffron threads

4   cups (1 liter) fish stock, hot

Salt and freshly ground black pepper

2   tablespoons finely chopped parsley

Lemon wedges, to serve

Preparation: 10 minutes
Cooking: 20 minutes

Serves: 4
Level: 1

CHORIZO AND CHICKEN PAELLA

Preheat the oven to 400°F (200°C/ gas 6). • Sauté the chicken and chorizo in 1 tablespoon oil in a paella pan or large frying pan over medium heat for 3 minutes until golden. • Add the onion, garlic, and bell peppers. Cook for 3 minutes. • Stir in the rice and peas. • Pour in the saffron stock and bring to a boil. Season with salt and pepper. • Cook over medium-high heat until all the liquid has almost been absorbed, about 10 minutes. The rice grains should still be slightly crunchy, and there should still be liquid in the pan. • Bake in the oven, uncovered, for 10 minutes. • Stir in the parsley and serve hot.

10	ounces (300 g) boneless, skinless chicken breasts, diced
2	dried chorizo sausages, sliced
2	tablespoons extra-virgin olive oil
1	onion, finely chopped
2	cloves garlic, finely chopped
1	small green bell pepper (capsicum), seeded and diced
1	small yellow bell pepper (capsicum), seeded and diced
2	cups (400 g) short-grain rice
1/2	cup (70 g) frozen peas, thawed
1/2	teaspoon saffron dissolved in 4 cups (1 liter) chicken stock, boiling
	Salt and freshly ground black pepper
2	tablespoons finely chopped fresh parsley

Preparation: 10 minutes
Cooking: 20 minutes

Serves: 4
Level: 1

ALMOND AND CURRANT PILAF WITH CHICKEN

Sauté the scallions, bell pepper, and garlic in 1 tablespoon of oil in a large saucepan over medium heat until softened, about 3 minutes. • Stir in the rice, turmeric, and peas. • Pour in the stock and bring to a boil. • Cover and simmer over low heat until the rice is tender and has absorbed almost all the liquid, 12–15 minutes. • Meanwhile, toast the almonds in a large frying pan until golden, 2–3 minutes. • Remove and set aside. • Sauté the chicken in the remaining oil in the same pan over medium heat until cooked through and golden, about 5 minutes. • Remove the rice from the heat and set aside. • Stir in the currants, almonds, and parsley. • Serve the pilaf hot with the chicken.

3   scallions (green onions), thinly sliced

1   red bell pepper (capsicum), seeded and diced

2   cloves garlic, finely chopped

2   tablespoons extra-virgin olive oil

$1^1/_2$ cups (300 g) basmati rice

$1/_2$ teaspoon ground turmeric

$2/_3$ cup (110 g) frozen peas, thawed

$2^1/_2$ cups (625 ml) chicken stock

$1/_2$ cup (75 g) slivered almonds

8   chicken tenders (tenderloins)

$1/_4$ cup (45 g) currants

2   tablespoons finely chopped fresh parsley

Preparation: 10 minutes
Cooking: 20–25 minutes

Serves: 4
Level: 1

CARROT, ZUCCHINI, AND CASHEW PILAF

Sauté the onion and garlic in the oil in a large saucepan over medium heat until softened, about 3 minutes. • Stir in the turmeric, cinnamon stick, and rice. • Pour in the stock. • Cover and simmer over low heat until the rice is tender and has absorbed almost all the liquid, 12–15 minutes. • Add the carrots and zucchini. Season with salt and pepper. • Discard the cinnamon stick. • Stir in the cashews. • Spoon into bowls. Garnish with the cilantro leaves and serve.

1	onion, finely chopped
2	cloves garlic, finely chopped
2	tablespoons extra-virgin olive oil
1	teaspoon ground turmeric
1	stick cinnamon
1^1/$_4$ cups (250 g)	basmati rice
1^1/$_2$ cups (375 ml)	vegetable stock, boiling
2	carrots, finely grated
2	zucchini (courgettes), finely grated
	Salt and freshly ground black pepper
^{1}/$_2$	cup (50 g) coarsely chopped roasted cashew nuts
4	sprigs fresh cilantro (coriander) leaves

Preparation: 10 minutes
Cooking: 14–17 minutes

Serves: 4
Level: 1

NASI GORENG

Cook the rice in a large saucepan of boiling water until tender, about 15 minutes. Drain well. • Meanwhile, place a wok over high heat. • When it is very hot, add 1 tablespoon of oil. • Lightly beat 2 of the eggs and stir-fry until scrambled and cooked, 1–2 minutes. • Remove from the wok and set aside. • Sauté the chicken in 1 tablespoon of oil in the same wok over medium heat until golden, about 3 minutes. • Add the scallions, cabbage, garlic, and carrots. Stir-fry for 2 minutes. • Stir in the cooked rice, scrambled eggs, and soy sauces. • Stir-fry for 2 minutes more. • Meanwhile, heat the remaining oil in a small frying pan. • Break the remaining 4 eggs into the pan and fry until cooked to your liking, 2–5 minutes. • Spoon the rice into 4 serving dishes and top each one with a fried egg. • Serve hot.

$1^{1}/_{2}$ cups (300 g) long-grain rice

3 tablespoons peanut oil

6 large eggs

1 pound (500 g) boneless, skinless chicken breasts, diced

3 scallions (green onions), thinly sliced

2 cups (200 g) finely shredded cabbage

2 cloves garlic, finely chopped

1 carrot, finely grated

2 tablespoons kecap manis (see page 274)

1 tablespoon dark soy sauce

4 large eggs

Preparation: 10 minutes
Cooking: 20 minutes

Serves: 4
Level: 1

RICE WITH HERB PESTO AND FETA

Cook the rice in a large saucepan of boiling water until tender, about 15 minutes. • Drain and rinse under cold water to stop the cooking process. • Meanwhile, put the herbs in the bowl of a food processor with the pine nuts, walnuts, chile, and garlic. Process for 15 seconds. • Transfer the herb pesto to a large bowl and stir in the oil. • Add the tomatoes and season with salt. • Add the rice to the tomato and pesto mixture. Stir in the feta. • Toss well and serve.

2 ounces (60 g) mixed fresh herbs (such as marjoram, parsley, thyme, chives, basil)

2 tablespoons pine nuts

12 walnuts

1 fresh red chile, seeded

1 clove garlic

1/4 cup (60 ml) extra-virgin olive oil

1 pound (500 g) cherry tomatoes, quartered

Salt

1 1/2 cups (300 g) long-grain rice

4 ounces (125 g) feta cheese, cut into small cubes

Preparation: 10 minutes

Cooking: 15 minutes

Serves: 4

Level: 1

BROWN RICE SALAD

Cook the rice in a large saucepan of boiling water, according to the instructions on the package. • Drain and rinse under ice-cold water to stop the cooking process. • Mix the rice, carrot, pea shoots, corn, scallions, and celery in a large bowl. • Mix the soy sauce, sesame oil, garlic, and ginger in a small bowl. • Pour the dressing over the rice and toss well. • Garnish with the cilantro and serve.

$1^1/_2$ cups (300 g) quick-cooking brown rice

1 carrot, peeled and finely grated

4 ounces (125 g) pea shoots or snow pea sprouts, trimmed and shredded

$2/_3$ cup (110 g) canned corn (sweet corn)

4 scallions (green onions), thinly sliced

2 sticks celery, thinly sliced

$1/_4$ cup (60 ml) light soy sauce

2 teaspoons Asian sesame oil

2 cloves garlic, finely chopped

2 teaspoons grated fresh ginger

Fresh cilantro (coriander) leaves, to serve

■■■ *Brown rice usually takes 35–40 minutes to cook. Quick-cooking brown rice is readily available in supermarkets and takes 10–15 minutes to cook. If preferred, replace the brown rice in this dish with the same quantity of short-grain white rice.*

Preparation: 10 minutes

Cooking: 10 minutes

Serves: 4

Level: 1

MEXICAN RICE IN TORTILLA CUPS

Preheat the oven to 425°F (220°C/gas 7). • Spray the tortillas with the oil and arrange them in 1-cup (250-ml) ramekins. • Bake for about 10 minutes, until crisp. • Meanwhile, cook the rice in a large saucepan of boiling water until tender, about 15 minutes. • Drain and set aside. • Sauté the chicken in the oil in a large frying pan over medium-high heat until golden, about 5 minutes. • Stir in the Cajun spices, scallions, and bell pepper. Cook for 3 minutes. • Add the rice, red kidney beans, peas, and corn. • Cook for 2 minutes. • Spoon the mixture into the tortilla cups. Top with the lettuce and ranch dressing.

4	**fajita-size flour tortillas**
	Olive oil spray
1	**cup (200 g) long-grain rice**
1	**pound (500 g) boneless, skinless chicken breasts, diced**
1	**tablespoon extra-virgin olive oil**
2	**teaspoons Cajun spices**
4	**scallions (green onions), thinly sliced**
1/2	**red bell pepper (capsicum), seeded and cubed**
1	**(14-ounce/400-g) can red kidney beans, drained and rinsed**
1/2	**cup (75 g) frozen peas**
1/2	**cup (60 g) canned corn (sweet corn)**
	Shredded lettuce and ranch dressing

Preparation: 10 minutes
Cooking: 20 minutes

Serves: 4
Level: 1

RICE WITH BEEF AND PINE NUTS

Sauté the onion, beef, and pine nuts in the oil in a large frying pan over medium-high heat for 4 minutes.
• Add the rice and water. • Bring to a boil. • Cover and simmer over low heat until the rice is tender and has absorbed almost all the liquid, 12–15 minutes.
• Stir in the oregano and season with salt and pepper. • Serve hot with the yogurt spooned over the top.

1   onion, finely chopped

1   pound (500 g) ground (minced) beef

1/2 cup (90 g) pine nuts

2   tablespoons extra-virgin olive oil

1 1/4 cups (250 g) basmati rice

2 1/2 cups (625 ml) water

2   tablespoons finely chopped fresh oregano

    Salt and freshly ground black pepper

1/3 cup (90 ml) plain yogurt

Preparation: 5 minutes
Cooking: 16–19 minutes

Serves: 2–4
Level: 1

TUNA COUSCOUS SALAD

Bring the water to a boil. • Stir in the couscous and 1 tablespoon of oil. • Cover and remove from the heat. • Let stand until the couscous has completely absorbed the liquid and is tender, about 10 minutes. • Transfer the couscous to a large bowl. • Fluff it up with a fork. • Add the onion, cucumber, tomatoes, olives, tuna, parsley, lemon juice, and the remaining oil. • Toss well and season with salt and pepper. • Serve with pita bread.

$1^1/4$ cups (300 ml) water

$1^1/4$ cups (250 g) instant couscous

$1/4$ cup (60 ml) extra-virgin olive oil

1 small red onion, thinly sliced

1 cucumber, thinly sliced

5 ounces (150 g) cherry tomatoes, halved

1 cup (100 g) pitted kalamata olives

2 cups (400 g) canned tuna, drained

3 tablespoons finely chopped fresh parsley

Freshly squeezed juice of 1 lemon

Salt and freshly ground black pepper

Pita bread, to serve

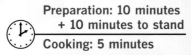

Preparation: 10 minutes + 10 minutes to stand

Cooking: 5 minutes

Serves: 4
Level: 1

SEAFOOD

SALT AND PEPPER SQUID

Cut the squid bodies in half lengthwise. Cut into squares and use a sharp knife to score the inside of the squid. • Crush the pepper in a pestle with a mortar until finely ground. • Mix the pepper, salt, and flour in a small bowl. • Heat the oil in a large frying pan until hot. Test the oil temperature by dropping a small piece of bread into the hot oil. If the bread immediately bubbles to the surface and begins to turn golden, the oil is ready.

• Dip the squid in the seasoned flour.

• Fry the squid in batches until golden and crisp, 2–3 minutes.

• Serve hot with the mixed salad greens, sweet chili sauce, and lemon wedges.

1³/4 pounds (800 g) squid, cleaned

1¹/2 tablespoons black peppercorns

1¹/2 tablespoons salt

¹/3 cup (50 g) all-purpose (plain) flour

4 cups (1 liter) olive oil, for frying

4 ounces (125 g) mixed salad greens

Thai sweet chili sauce, to serve

Lemon wedges, to serve

Preparation: 15 minutes
Cooking: 10 minutes

Serves: 4
Level: 1

SEAFOOD KEBABS WITH CREAMY ANISEED SAUCE

Bring a large saucepan of salted water to a boil. • Add the rice and cook over medium heat for 10–15 minutes, until tender. • Drain well and set aside.
• Preheat a broiler (grill). • Mix 2 tablespoons of oil, the lemon zest, and 1 tablespoon of lemon juice in a small bowl. Season with salt and pepper.
• Thread the shrimp and tuna onto skewers and place them on a plate. Drizzle with the oil mixture. • Mix the cream, anisette, remaining lemon juice, remaining oil, paprika, and dill in a small bowl. Season with salt and pepper.
• Broil the kebabs, turning them often, for 5 minutes, or until cooked through.
• Arrange the rice on serving dishes and top with the kebabs. • Drizzle the kebabs with the sauce and serve hot.

2	cups (400 g) basmati rice
3	tablespoons extra-virgin olive oil
	Finely grated zest and juice of 1 lemon
	Salt and freshly ground black pepper
12	large shrimp (prawn)
1	pound (500 g) tuna steak, cut into small chunks
1	cup (250 ml) heavy (double) cream
1	tablespoon anisette (aniseed liqueur)
1/2	teaspoon sweet paprika
2	tablespoons finely chopped fresh dill

Preparation: 10 minutes
Cooking: 15 minutes

Serves: 4
Level: 1

TUNA STEAKS WITH ORANGE AND CAPERS

Preheat a broiler (grill). • Use a sharp knife to cut the zest from the oranges in very fine strips. • Blanch the zest in boiling water for 2 minutes. • Drain and set aside. • Arrange the fennel, radishes, celery, tomatoes, olives, and salad greens in a large salad bowl. • Add the chervil, dill, and orange zest. Drizzle with half the oil and the vinegar. Season with salt and pepper and toss well. • Squeeze the juice from the oranges into a small bowl. Season with salt and pepper. • Gradually beat in the remaining oil until well blended. • Stir in the capers. • Broil the tuna steaks for about 5 minutes, turning them occasionally, until cooked through. • Place the salad on a large serving plate. • Arrange the tuna steaks on top and drizzle with the orange and caper dressing. • Serve hot.

2	large ripe oranges
1	bulb fennel, thinly sliced
4	radishes, thinly sliced
1	stalk celery, thinly sliced
4	cherry tomatoes, cut into wedges
1	cup (100 g) black olives
10	ounces (300 g) mixed salad greens
1	sprig chervil, finely chopped
1	sprig dill, finely chopped
1/3	cup (90 ml) extra-virgin olive oil
3	tablespoons balsamic vinegar
	Salt and freshly ground black pepper
1/3	cup (60 g) capers in brine, rinsed and drained
4	tuna steaks

 Preparation: 15 minutes
Cooking: 7 minutes

Serves: 4
Level: 1

SNAPPER FILLETS WITH AVOCADO SALSA

To prepare the snapper fillets, place a grill pan over medium-high heat. • Mix the potatoes with 1 tablespoon of oil. Season with salt and pepper. • Grill the potatoes, turning them from time to time, until cooked, about 10 minutes. • Brush the snapper fillets with the remaining oil. Season with salt and pepper. • Grill the fish until cooked, about 3 minutes on each side. • To prepare the avocado salsa, mix the avocado, cucumber, tomato, and onion in a medium bowl. • Add the lemon juice, white wine vinegar, cilantro, and sugar. Toss well. • Arrange the potatoes on individual serving plates. Top with the fish and avocado salsa.

Snapper Fillets

2   large potatoes, very thinly sliced

2   tablespoons extra-virgin olive oil

    Salt and freshly ground black pepper

4   snapper fillets, each weighing about 6 ounces (180 g)

Avocado Salsa

1   avocado, peeled and diced

1   small cucumber, diced

1   tomato, diced

1/2   small red onion, finely chopped

2   tablespoons freshly squeezed lemon juice

2   tablespoons white wine vinegar

1/3   cup (20 g) fresh cilantro (coriander)

1/8   teaspoon superfine (caster) sugar

Preparation: 15 minutes

Cooking: 16 minutes

Serves: 4

Level: 1

SOLE BAKED WITH CHERRY TOMATOES

Preheat the oven to 350°F (180°C/gas 4).
• Grease a large baking dish with oil.
• Drizzle each fillet with a little oil.
• Arrange the sole in the prepared dish.
• Top with the tomatoes, garlic, and parsley. Season with salt and pepper. Drizzle with the remaining oil. • Bake for 10–15 minutes, until the sole and tomatoes are cooked. • Serve hot.

8   sole fillets

1/4 cup (60 ml) extra-virgin olive oil

1   pound (500 g) cherry tomatoes, halved

4   cloves garlic, finely chopped

2   tablespoons finely chopped fresh parsley

    Salt and freshly ground black pepper

Preparation: 10 minutes
Cooking: 10–15 minutes

Serves: 4
Level: 1

PERCH WITH CHERRY TOMATOES AND OLIVES

Sauté the onions in the oil in a large frying pan over medium heat for about 3 minutes, until softened. • Add the perch and cook for 2 minutes. Turn the fish over and cook for 2 more minutes. • Add the tomatoes and olives. Cook for 3 minutes. • Pour in the beer and let it evaporate for 2 minutes. • Pour in the stock and cook for 5 minutes. • Season with salt and pepper and garnish with the basil. • Serve hot.

2   small onions, finely chopped

3   tablespoons extra-virgin olive oil

2   pounds (1 kg) perch fillets

1   pound (500 g) cherry tomatoes, halved

1   cup (100 g) black olives, pitted and cut in half

1/2   cup (125 ml) beer

1/3   cup (90 ml) fish or vegetable stock

Salt and freshly ground black pepper

Basil leaves, to garnish

Preparation: 10 minutes
Cooking: 17 minutes

Serves: 4–6
Level: 1

COD WITH POTATOES

Sauté the onion in the oil and butter in a large frying pan over medium heat until softened, about 3 minutes • Add the potatoes and sauté for 5 minutes. • Add the fish, rosemary, and lemon zest.
• Pour in the milk and enough water to cover the ingredients. Season with salt and pepper. • Simmer until the fish and potatoes are tender and the sauce has reduced to half its original volume, 5–10 minutes. • Sprinkle with the parsley and garnish with sprigs of rosemary.
• Serve hot.

1	large onion, cut into rings
2	tablespoons extra-virgin olive oil
1	tablespoon butter
2	pounds (1 kg) potatoes, peeled, and cut into thin wedges
1¼	pounds (600 g) cod, hake, or other white-flesh fish fillets
1	tablespoon finely chopped rosemary + extra sprigs, to garnish
	Zest of ¹/2 lemon, very finely cut
¹/4	cup (60 ml) milk
¹/2	cup (125 ml) water
	Salt and freshly ground black pepper
1	tablespoon finely chopped fresh parsley

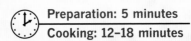

Preparation: 5 minutes
Cooking: 12–18 minutes

Serves: 4
Level: 1

PARMESAN-CRUMBED BAKED SALMON

Preheat the oven to 400°F (200°C/gas 6). Line a baking sheet with parchment paper. • Combine the bread crumbs, parsley, Parmesan, lemon zest, salt, and pepper in a bowl. • Drizzle with the oil. Stir until the bread crumbs are lightly coated in oil. • Press the bread crumb mixture onto the flesh-side of the fish to form an even topping. • Place the fish, skin-side down, on the prepared baking sheet. Spray liberally with oil. • Roast the fish about 12–15 minutes, until the bread crumbs are lightly golden and fish is just cooked through. • Serve hot with a leafy green salad and lemon wedges.

$1/2$ cup (30 g) fresh multigrain bread crumbs

$1/4$ cup finely chopped flat-leaf parsley leaves

2 ounces (60 g) freshly grated Parmesan cheese

1 teaspoon finely grated lemon zest

Salt and freshly ground black pepper

2 tablespoons extra-virgin olive oil

4 (8-ounce/250-g) salmon or ocean trout fillets

Olive oil cooking spray

Leafy green salad, to serve

Lemon wedges, to serve

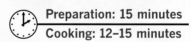

Preparation: 15 minutes
Cooking: 12–15 minutes

Serves: 4
Level: 1

CHERMOULA FISH WITH COUSCOUS

To make the chermoula, combine the cilantro, cumin, cayenne pepper, paprika, garlic, 4 tablespoons of oil, lemon juice, salt, and pepper in a food processor. Process until well combined. • Pour the mixture into a shallow dish. • Add the fish to the chermoula. Turn the fish to coat well in the chermoula. • Set aside for 10 minutes. • Meanwhile, put the couscous in a heatproof bowl. Pour the boiling water over the top. Cover and set aside until the water is absorbed, about 5 minutes. Stir with a fork to separate grains. • Stir in 3 tablespoons of oil and season with salt and pepper. • Add the tomatoes. Set aside. • Heat the remaining oil in a large frying pan over medium-high heat. • Cook the fish until just tender, 3–5 minutes on each side. • Serve hot with the couscous and lemon wedges.

- 1 cup (50 g) fresh cilantro (coriander)
- 1 teaspoon ground cumin
- 1/4 teaspoon cayenne pepper
- 1 teaspoon paprika
- 2 cloves garlic, crushed
- 1/2 cup (120 ml) extra-virgin olive oil
- 3 tablespoons freshly squeezed lemon juice
  Salt and freshly ground black pepper
- 4 firm white fish steaks, such as cod, snapper, ling, or warehou
- 1 3/4 cups (350 g) instant couscous
- 2 cups (500 ml) water, boiling
- 8 ounces (250 g) cherry tomatoes, chopped
  Lemon wedges, to serve

■■■ *Chermoula is a North African marinade used to flavor fish or seafood. It is usually made from a mixture of olive oil, lemon juice, garlic, and herbs.*

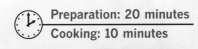

Preparation: 20 minutes

Cooking: 10 minutes

Serves: 4
Level: 1

FISH, BELL PEPPER, AND RED ONION SKEWERS

Place the fish in a shallow dish. Combine the oil, lemon juice, oregano, salt, and pepper in a screw-top jar. Shake until well combined. • Pour the oil and lemon mixture over the fish. Toss to coat well. Set aside for 5 minutes. • Thread the fish, bell pepper, and onion alternately onto presoaked bamboo skewers. • Preheat a lightly oiled grill on medium-high heat. • Grill the skewers, turning frequently and brushing with the remaining marinade, until the fish is cooked through, 5–8 minutes. • Serve the skewers hot with the tartar sauce and lemon wedges.

$1^1/_2$ **pounds (750 g) firm white fish fillets, skinned and cut into into 1-inch (2.5-cm) cubes**

$1/_3$ **cup (90 ml) extra-virgin olive oil**

Freshly squeezed juice of 2 lemons

2 **teaspoons dried oregano**

Salt and freshly ground black pepper

1 **red bell pepper (capsicum), trimmed, seeded and cut into 1-inch (2.5-cm) pieces**

2 **small red onions, cut into thin wedges**

Tartar sauce and lemon wedges, to serve

■■■ *You will need 12 presoaked bamboo skewers to prepare this dish.*

Preparation: 20 minutes

Cooking: 5–8 minutes

Serves: 4

Level: 1

FISH, FENNEL, AND MUSSEL STEW

Heat the oil in a large deep frying pan over medium-high heat. • Sauté the garlic and fennel until softened, about 3 minutes. • Add the stock and wine to the pan. Simmer over medium-low heat until reduced by half. • Stir in the tomato sauce, sugar, bay leaves, and saffron. Season with salt and pepper. Cover and bring to a boil. Stir in the fish. • Cover and cook for 2 minutes. Add the mussels and cook until opened and the fish is just tender, 2–3 minutes. • Discard any unopened mussels. • Sprinkle with the reserved chopped fennel leaves. • Serve hot with mashed potatoes.

1 tablespoon extra-virgin olive oil

3 cloves garlic, crushed

1 fennel bulb, halved and thinly sliced (reserve leaves)

1/2 cup (125 ml) fish stock or clam juice

1/3 cup (90 ml) dry white wine

3 cups (750 ml) tomato pasta sauce

1/2 teaspoon superfine (caster) sugar

2 bay leaves

1/4 teaspoon saffron threads soaked in 1 tablespoon water

Salt and freshly ground black pepper

1 1/2 pounds (750 g) firm white fish fillets, skinned and cubed

12 mussels, scrubbed and beards removed

Mashed potatoes, to serve

Preparation: 15 minutes
Cooking: 6 minutes

Serves: 4
Level: 1

SPICY LIME AND CILANTRO FISH PACKAGES

Preheat the oven to 400°F (200°C/gas 6). • Spray four 12 x 16-inch (30 x 40-cm) sheets of parchment paper with nonstick cooking spray. • Score the thickest part of the fish twice. Place a fillet in the center of each sheet of parchment paper. • Combine the cilantro, sugar, fish sauce, lime juice, and sweet chili sauce in a small bowl. • Drizzle over the fish. Top the fish with the scallions. • Fold the paper and wrap the fish to form secure packages. • Place the packages folded side up on a baking sheet. • Bake for 10–15 minutes (timing will depend on the thickness of the packages), until the fish is just cooked through when tested with a skewer. • Open the packages and top with cilantro. Serve with the lime wedges and steamed jasmine rice.

4	(8-ounce/250-g) salmon or ocean trout fillets
1/4	cup coarsely chopped cilantro (coriander) leaves + extra leaves, to garnish
1	tablespoon light brown sugar
1	teaspoon Asian fish sauce
1/4	cup (60 ml) freshly squeezed lime juice
3	tablespoons Thai sweet chili sauce
3	scallions (green onions), thinly sliced diagonally
	Lime wedges, to serve
	Steamed jasmine rice, to serve

Preparation: 15 minutes
Cooking: 10–15 minutes

Serves: 4
Level: 1

CRISP BATTERED FISH WITH LEMON AND DILL MAYONNAISE

Combine the mayonnaise, lemon zest and juice, and dill in a bowl. Season with salt and pepper. Stir to combine. Chill until ready to serve. • To make the batter, place the flour in a bowl. Gradually whisk in enough beer to form a smooth batter. Set aside. • Heat the oil in deep-fryer until hot. Test the oil temperature by dropping a small piece of bread into the hot oil. If the bread immediately bubbles to the surface and begins to trun golden, the oil is ready. • Dust the fish in cornstarch and dip in the batter, draining off any excess. • Deep-fry the fish in batches until golden brown and just cooked through, 2–3 minutes. Drain on paper towels. • Serve hot with the lemon wedges and lemon and dill mayonnaise.

1	cup (250 ml) mayonnaise
2	teaspoons finely grated lemon zest
1	tablespoon freshly squeezed lemon juice
1	tablespoon finely chopped fresh dill leaves
	Salt and freshly ground black pepper
1	cup (150 g) all-purpose (plain) flour
	About $3/4$ cup (180 ml) chilled beer
4	cups (1 liter) vegetable oil, for frying
8	(5-ounce/150-g) skinless firm white fish fillets such as whiting, snapper, or hake
1	tablespoon cornstarch (cornflour)
	Lemon wedges, to serve

Preparation: 15 minutes
Cooking: 6 minutes

Serves: 4
Level: 1

GRILLED TUNA WITH TOMATO AND MOZZARELLA SALAD

To make the salad, combine the tomatoes, olives, onion, mozzarella, and parsley in a bowl. Season with salt and pepper. • Drizzle with 2 tablespoons of the oil and the balsamic vinegar. Toss to combine. Set aside. • Preheat a grill on high. • Brush both sides of the tuna steaks with the remaining oil. Season with salt and pepper. • Grill the tuna until half cooked through, 2–3 minutes on each side (tuna can be served slightly raw in the center). • Place the tuna on serving plates. Top with the tomato salad and arugula leaves and serve hot.

8 ounces (250 g) cherry tomatoes, chopped

2 ounces (60 g) pitted black olives, chopped

1/2 small red onion, halved and very thinly sliced

4 mozzarella balls (bocconcini), chopped

2 tablespoons coarsely chopped flat-leaf parsley

Salt and freshly ground black pepper

1/4 cup (60 ml) extra-virgin olive oil

2 tablespoons balsamic vinegar

4 6-ounce (180-g) tuna steaks

Arugula (rocket) leaves, to serve

 Preparation: 15 minutes
Cooking: 4–6 minutes

Serves: 4
Level: 1

POULTRY

CHICKEN, LEEK, AND MUSHROOM PIES

Preheat the oven to 425°F (220°C/gas 7).
• Sauté the chicken in the oil in a large,
deep frying pan over medium-high heat
until cooked, about 3 minutes. • Add the
leeks and mushrooms. Cover and simmer
for 3 minutes. • Stir in the sour cream,
mustard, and thyme. Season with salt
and pepper. • Spoon the mixture evenly
into four 1-cup (250-ml) ramekins. • Cut
the pastry into four squares and place
over the tops of the ramekins. • Brush
the pastry with the beaten egg. • Bake
for 8–10 minutes until puffed and golden.
• Serve hot.

$1^1/2$ pounds (750 g)
    boneless, skinless
    chicken breasts, cut
    into small cubes

2   tablespoons extra-
    virgin olive oil

2   leeks, halved
    lengthwise
    and thinly sliced

8   ounces (250 g)
    mushrooms,
    quartered

1   cup (250 ml)
    sour cream

1   tablespoon
    Dijon mustard

2   tablespoons finely
    chopped fresh
    thyme

    Salt and freshly
    ground black pepper

8   ounces (250 g)
    frozen puff pastry,
    thawed

1   large egg,
    lightly beaten

Preparation: 10 minutes

Cooking: 14–16 minutes

Serves: 4
Level: 1

GRILLED CHICKEN WITH GARLIC, LEMON, AND PARSLEY

210

Mix the oil, lemon zest and juice, garlic, and parsley in a small dish. • Add the chicken and coat well. Season with salt and pepper. • Place a grill pan over medium-high heat. • Grill the chicken until cooked through, about 5 minutes on each side. • Serve the chicken hot with the arugula and tomatoes.

2   tablespoons extra-virgin olive oil

Finely grated zest and juice of 1 lemon

2   cloves garlic, finely chopped

2   tablespoons finely chopped fresh parsley

3   boneless, skinless chicken breasts, halved lengthwise

Salt and freshly ground black pepper

8   ounces (250 g) arugula (rocket)

4   tomatoes, cut into wedges

 Preparation: 10 minutes
Cooking: 10 minutes

Serves: 4
Level: 1

GREEK CHICKEN KEBABS WITH TZATZIKI

To prepare the chicken kebabs, thread the chicken onto presoaked bamboo skewers. • Mix the oil, lemon juice, garlic, and oregano in a small dish. Season with salt and pepper. • Add the chicken skewers and coat well. • To prepare the tzatziki, mix the yogurt, lemon juice, cucumber, and mint in a small bowl. • Place a grill pan over medium-high heat. • Grill the kebabs, turning them from time to time, until cooked through, 6–8 minutes. • Serve the chicken kebabs with the tzatziki, tomatoes, lettuce, and pita bread.

Preparation: 15 minutes
Cooking: 6–8 minutes

Serves: 4
Level: 1

Chicken Kebabs

1 3/4 pounds (800 g) boneless, skinless chicken, cut into small cubes

1/4 cup (60 ml) extra-virgin olive oil

2 tablespoons freshly squeezed lemon juice

2 cloves garlic, finely chopped

2 teaspoons dried oregano

Salt and freshly ground black pepper

Tzatziki

3/4 cup (180 ml) plain yogurt

2 tablespoons freshly squeezed lemon juice

1 small cucumber, finely grated

2 tablespoons finely chopped fresh mint

To Serve

2 tomatoes, diced

Finely shredded lettuce, to serve

Pita bread, to serve

LIME AND CILANTRO CHICKEN KEBABS

214

Bring a large saucepan of salted water to a boil. • Add the rice and cook over medium heat until tender, 10–15 minutes. Drain well. • Thread the chicken onto presoaked bamboo skewers. • Mix the sweet chili sauce, lime juice, soy sauce, and cilantro in a small bowl. • Add the chicken skewers and coat well. • Place a grill pan over medium-high heat. • Grill the chicken until cooked, about 3 minutes on each side. • Serve the kebabs with the rice and baby Asian salad greens.

2	cups (400 g) jasmine rice
3	boneless, skinless chicken breasts, trimmed
2	tablespoons Thai sweet chili sauce
2	tablespoons freshly squeezed lime juice
1	tablespoon light soy sauce
1	tablespoon finely chopped fresh cilantro (coriander)
4	ounces (125 g) baby Asian greens

Preparation: 10 minutes
Cooking: 16–21 minutes

Serves: 4
Level: 1

JAPANESE-STYLE CHICKEN WITH RICE

Bring a large saucepan of salted water to a boil. • Add the rice and cook over medium heat until tender, 12–15 minutes. • Drain and rinse under ice-cold water to stop the cooking process. • Mix 2 tablespoons of peanut oil, the soy sauce, mirin, ginger, and half the garlic in a small dish. • Add the chicken and coat well. • Place a grill pan over medium-high heat. • Grill the chicken until cooked, about 3 minutes on each side. • Meanwhile, heat 2 teaspoons of oil in a wok or large frying pan over medium heat. • Add the eggs and stir-fry until scrambled, about 1 minute. • Remove from the pan and set aside. • Sauté the scallions and remaining garlic in the remaining oil in the same pan for about 1 minute until softened. • Add the rice and return the eggs to the wok. • Stir-fry for 1 minute. • Serve the chicken hot with rice.

1^1/4 cups (250 g) long-grain rice

^{1}/4 cup (60 ml) peanut oil

^{1}/4 cup (60 ml) light soy sauce

^{1}/4 cup (60 ml) mirin or sweet sherry

2 teaspoons finely grated fresh ginger

4 cloves garlic, finely chopped

3 boneless, skinless chicken breasts, halved

2 large eggs, lightly beaten

4 scallions (green onions), thinly sliced

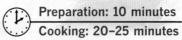

Preparation: 10 minutes
Cooking: 20–25 minutes

Serves: 4
Level: 1

MOROCCAN CHICKEN WITH CORN SALSA

Mix the ras el hanout with the oil in a small bowl. • Brush the chicken with the mixture. • Place a grill pan over medium-high heat. • Grill the chicken until cooked, about 3 minutes on each side. • To prepare the salsa, mix the corn, tomatoes, cucumber, onion, lemon juice, cilantro, and oil in a small bowl. • Season with salt and pepper. • Serve the chicken hot with the salsa.

■■■ *Ras el hanout is a blend of up to 30 different Moroccan spices. It has a subtle yet fiery kick and is used to add nuance and flavor to many different dishes. It is available at African foodstores and online.*

2   teaspoons ras el hanout (mixed Moroccan spices)

2   tablespoons extra-virgin olive oil

4   small boneless, skinless chicken breasts, halved

Salsa

2   cups (250 g) canned corn (sweet corn), drained

2   tomatoes, diced

1   cucumber, diced

1   small red onion, finely chopped

2   tablespoons freshly squeezed lemon juice

2   tablespoons finely chopped fresh cilantro (coriander)

2   tablespoons extra-virgin olive oil

Salt and freshly ground black pepper

 Preparation: 10 minutes
Cooking: 6 minutes

Serves: 4
Level: 1

HERB-CRUMBED CHICKEN

Flatten the chicken with a meat tenderizer. • Mix the bread crumbs, parsley, and chives in a small bowl. Season with salt and pepper. • Dip the chicken first in the flour, then in the beaten eggs, followed by the herbed bread crumbs. • Fry the chicken in batches in the oil in a large frying pan over medium heat until golden and crisp, about 2 minutes on each side. • Serve the chicken with the lemon wedges and French fries.

4	small boneless, skinless chicken breasts
2	cups (120 g) fresh bread crumbs
2	tablespoons finely chopped fresh parsley
2	tablespoons finely chopped fresh chives
	Salt and freshly ground black pepper
1/4	cup (30 g) all-purpose (plain) flour
2	large eggs, lightly beaten
2	tablespoons extra-virgin olive oil
	Lemon wedges and chips, to serve
	French fries (potato chips), to serve

Preparation: 15 minutes
Cooking: 8 minutes

Serves: 4
Level: 1

CHICKEN BURGERS
WITH OLIVE BUTTER

Process $1/2$ cup (60 g) of olives in a food processor until smooth. • Mix the butter, olive paste, and garlic in a small bowl. • Place the mixture on a sheet of aluminum foil and shape into a log. Wrap in the foil and place in the freezer. • Meanwhile, place the chicken in a medium bowl. Stir in the shallot and thyme. Season with salt and pepper. • Divide the chicken mixture into 6–8 portions and shape into burgers. • Fry the burgers in the oil in a large frying pan over medium-high heat until cooked, about 4 minutes on each side. • Arrange the burgers on a bed of arugula and garnish with the remaining olives. • Slice the frozen butter and place on top of the burgers. • Serve hot.

$3/4$ cup (90 g) pitted black olives

$1/2$ cup (125 g) butter at room temperature

1 clove garlic, finely chopped

2 pounds (1 kg) ground (minced) chicken

1 shallot, finely chopped

3 tablespoons finely chopped fresh thyme

Salt and freshly ground black pepper

$1/4$ cup (60 ml) extra-virgin olive oil

1 bunch arugula (rocket), to serve

Preparation: 15 minutes
Cooking: 8 minutes

Serves: 4–6
Level: 1

CITRUS CHICKEN WITH FETA AND ARUGULA

Heat the oil in a large frying pan over medium-high heat. Sauté the chicken, turning once, until golden, about 10 minutes. • Add the onion and sauté until just tender, about 3 minutes. • Add the orange and lemon juice. Cover and bring to a boil. Sprinkle with the olives and feta. Cover and cook for 1 minute.

• Arrange the chicken on serving plates, drizzle with the pan juices and serve hot with the arugula.

3	tablespoons extra-virgin olive oil
6	boneless chicken thighs, with skin, halved
2	red onions, thinly sliced
	Freshly squeezed juice of 1 orange
	Freshly squeezed juice of 1 lemon
3/4	cup (90 g) pitted black olives
3	ounces (90 g) feta cheese, crumbled
1	bunch arugula (rocket), trimmed

Preparation: 10 minutes
Cooking: 12 minutes

Serves: 4
Level: 1

GLAZED CHICKEN WINGS WITH POTATO WEDGES

Preheat the oven to 450°F (230°C/gas 8).
• Line two large baking sheets with
parchment paper. • Combine the tomato,
barbecue, and Worcestershire sauces,
brown sugar, and paprika in a large bowl.
Season with salt and pepper. • Add the
chicken. Toss to coat in the mixture.
• Place the chicken in a single layer
on one baking sheet. Place the potato
wedges on the other baking sheet.
• Roast the chicken and potato wedges
for about 20 minutes, turning once, until
crisp and golden. • Serve hot with the
green salad.

$1/3$ cup (90 ml) tomato
      sauce

$1/3$ cup (90 ml)
      barbecue sauce

1   tablespoon
      Worcestershire
      sauce

$1/3$ cup (70 g) firmly
      packed brown sugar

$1/2$ teaspoon ground
      paprika

      Salt and freshly
      ground black pepper

12   large chicken wings,
      cut in three pieces
      (discard wing tips)

1   pound (500 g)
      frozen potato
      wedges

      Leafy green salad,
      to serve

Preparation: 10 minutes

Cooking: 20 minutes

Serves: 4
Level: 1

DUCK AND SCALLION YAKITORI

Presoak 12 bamboo skewers. • To make the yakitori sauce, combine the soy sauce, stock, mirin, and sugar in a saucepan. Bring to a boil, stirring from time to time, over high heat. • Reduce the heat and simmer until the sauce is reduced by about one-third, about 5 minutes. • Set aside to cool slightly. Pour into a shallow ceramic dish. • Divide the ingredients evenly, and thread the duck and scallion (crosswise) onto the skewers. • Place the skewers in the yakitori sauce. Turn to coat in the sauce. • Preheat a lightly oiled grill on medium-high heat. • Grill the skewers, basting with the yakitori sauce from time to time, until just cooked through, 8–10 minutes. • Serve hot with the rice.

$1/2$ cup (125 ml) reduced salt soy sauce

$1/3$ cup (90 ml) chicken stock

$1/4$ cup (60 ml) mirin

$1/4$ cup (50 g) superfine (caster) sugar

$1^{3}/_{4}$ pounds (800 g) boneless duck breasts, trimmed and cut into 1-inch (2.5-cm) pieces

8 scallions (green onions), trimmed and cut into 2-inch (5-cm) lengths

Steamed short grain rice, to serve

Preparation: 15 minutes
Cooking: 8–15 minutes

Serves: 4
Level: 1

SAGE-CRUMBED TURKEY WITH SWEET POTATOES

Combine the bread crumbs and sage in a shallow dish. Season with salt and pepper. • Lightly coat the turkey with flour and egg. Lightly press the crumb mixture over the turkey. • Cook the sweet potatoes in a saucepan of boiling water until tender, about 10 minutes. • Drain and return to the saucepan. Mash briefly. Add the milk, butter, and nutmeg. Season with salt and pepper. Mash until smooth. • Meanwhile, heat the oil in a frying pan over medium heat. Cook the turkey in batches until golden and crisp, about 2 minutes on each side. Drain on paper towels. • Serve the turkey with the sweet potatoes.

$1^1/_2$ cups (120 g) fresh bread crumbs

$^1/_4$ cup finely chopped fresh sage leaves

Salt and freshly ground black pepper

4 turkey breast fillets

2 tablespoons all-purpose (plain) flour

2 large eggs, lightly beaten

$1^3/_4$ pounds (800 g) sweet potatoes, peeled and cut into large chunks

$^1/_3$ cup (90 ml) milk, hot

2 tablespoons butter, diced

Pinch ground nutmeg

2 tablespoons extra-virgin olive oil

Preparation: 15 minutes

Cooking: 10 minutes

Serves: 4

Level: 1

GRUYÈRE ROAST CHICKEN WITH SPINACH

Preheat the oven to 400°F (200°C/gas 6). • Line a baking sheet with parchment paper. • Make a slit lengthwise through each chicken breast to form a pocket (do not cut all the way through). • Stuff the cheese and chives inside each pocket. • Heat the oil in a frying pan over medium-high heat. • Sauté the chicken in batches until golden, about 2 minutes each side. • Transfer the chicken to the baking sheet. Roast for 6–8 minutes, until just cooked through. Cover and let rest for 5 minutes. • Meanwhile, heat the butter in the frying pan over medium heat. Sauté the spinach until just wilted, 2–3 minutes. Season with salt, pepper, and nutmeg. • Serve the chicken hot with the spinach.

4	boneless, skinless chicken breast fillets
5	ounces (150 g) Gruyère cheese, thinly sliced
2	tablespoons finely chopped fresh chives
1	tablespoon extra-virgin olive oil
1/3	cup (90 g) butter
1	bunch spinach, trimmed
	Salt and freshly ground black pepper
	Pinch ground nutmeg

Preparation: 15 minutes
Cooking: 12 minutes

Serves: 4
Level: 1

MEAT

GROUND BEEF WITH VEGETABLES AND MASHED POTATO

Cook the potatoes in a large saucepan of boiling water until tender, 10 minutes. • Drain well and return to the pan. • Add the butter and milk. Mash until smooth. Season with salt and pepper. • Meanwhile, sauté the onion and garlic in the oil in a large frying pan over medium-low heat until softened, about 3 minutes. • Add the beef and sauté until browned, about 5 minutes. • Stir in the tomatoes. Bring to a boil. • Cover and simmer over low heat until thickened, about 5 minutes. • Add the vegetables and simmer for 5 minutes. • Season with salt and pepper. • Serve the beef hot with the mashed potato. Garnish with the parsley.

1	pound (500 g) potatoes, peeled and diced
2	tablespoons butter
2	tablespoons milk
	Salt and freshly ground black pepper
1	onion, finely chopped
2	cloves garlic, finely chopped
1	tablespoon extra-virgin olive oil
1	pound (500 g) ground (minced) beef
2	cups (500 ml) chopped tomatoes
1	cup (150 g) frozen mixed peas, carrots, and corn
	Sprigs of parsley, to garnish

Preparation: 10 minutes
Cooking: 20 minutes

Serves: 4
Level: 1

BEEF SIRLOIN WITH TOMATO AND OLIVE SAUCE

Cook the potatoes in a large saucepan of boiling water until tender, 10–15 minutes. • Drain well. • Meanwhile, sauté the onion and garlic in 1 tablespoon of oil in a large frying pan over medium-low heat until softened, about 3 minutes. • Stir in the tomatoes, olives, and sugar. Simmer over low heat until thickened, about 4 minutes. • Add the oregano and season with salt and pepper. • Heat the remaining oil in a large frying pan over medium-high heat. • Sauté the steaks for about 4 minutes on each side, or until cooked to your liking. • Serve the steaks hot with the sauce and potatoes.

$1^1/_2$ pounds (750 g) new potatoes, halved

1 red onion, thinly sliced

2 cloves garlic, finely chopped

2 tablespoons extra-virgin olive oil

$1^1/_2$ cups (375 ml) chopped tomatoes

$^2/_3$ cup (60 g) pitted kalamata olives

1 teaspoon sugar

2 tablespoons finely chopped fresh oregano

Salt and freshly ground black pepper

4 sirloin steaks

Preparation: 10 minutes
Cooking: 20 minutes

Serves: 4
Level: 1

BEEF STEAKS WITH MUSHROOMS AND SWEET POTATOES

Cook the sweet potatoes in a large saucepan of boiling water until tender, 10–15 minutes. • Drain well and return to the pan. • Add the butter and milk. Mash until smooth. Season with salt and pepper. • Meanwhile, sauté the mushrooms, scallions, and garlic in 2 tablespoons of oil in a large frying pan over medium heat until softened, about 3 minutes. • Stir in the cream, lemon juice, and thyme. • Bring to a boil. Simmer over low heat until thickened, about 1 minute. • Heat the remaining oil in a large frying pan over medium-high heat. • Sauté the steaks for about 4 minutes on each side, or until cooked to your liking. • Serve the steaks hot with the mushroom sauce and sweet potatoes.

$1^{1}/_{2}$ pounds (750 g) sweet potatoes, peeled and diced

2 tablespoons butter

$^{1}/_{4}$ cup (60 ml) milk

Salt and freshly ground black pepper

8 ounces (250 g) mushrooms, thinly sliced

4 scallions (green onions), thinly sliced

2 cloves garlic, finely chopped

$^{1}/_{4}$ cup (60 ml) extra-virgin olive oil

1 cup (250 ml) light (single) cream

3 tablespoons freshly squeezed lemon juice

1 tablespoon fresh thyme leaves

4 beef fillet steaks

Preparation: 15 minutes
Cooking: 15 minutes

Serves: 4
Level: 1

FILLET STEAK WITH BÉARNAISE SAUCE

To prepare the béarnaise sauce, place the egg yolks, vinegar, and water in a double boiler over barely simmering water. Heat until the mixture reaches 160°F (80°C) and is light and fluffy. • Let cool a little, then gradually pour in the butter, mixing until thick and smooth. • Stir in the tarragon and season with salt and pepper. • Mix the potatoes with 1 tablespoon of oil in a large bowl and season with salt and pepper. • Season the steaks with salt and pepper and drizzle with the remaining oil. • Place a grill pan over medium-high heat. • Grill the potatoes until cooked, 4–5 minutes each side. • Set aside. • Sauté the steaks for about 4 minutes on each side, or until cooked to your liking.
• Serve the steaks hot with the potatoes, spinach, and béarnaise sauce.

4 large egg yolks

2 tablespoons white wine vinegar

2 tablespoons water

1/2 cup (125 g) butter, melted

1 tablespoon finely chopped fresh tarragon

Salt and freshly ground black pepper

11/2 pounds (750 g) potatoes, unpeeled, thinly sliced diagonally

2 tablespoons extra-virgin olive oil

4 beef fillet steaks

5 ounces (150 g) baby spinach leaves, to serve

Preparation: 10 minutes
Cooking: 20 minutes

Serves: 4
Level: 1

GREEK BEEF KEBABS

Mix the beef, bread crumbs, egg, feta, garlic, onion, cumin, lemon zest, parsley, and oregano in a large bowl. • Shape the mixture into eight long sausages. • Thread the sausages onto metal skewers. • Place a grill pan over medium-high heat. • Grill the kebabs until cooked to your liking, turning from time to time, 6–8 minutes. • Serve the kebabs hot with the tomatoes and salad.

$1^1/2$ pounds (750 g) ground (minced) beef

1 cup (60 g) fresh bread crumbs

1 large egg, lightly beaten

4 ounces (125 g) feta cheese, crumbled

2 cloves garlic, finely chopped

2 tablespoons grated red onion

2 teaspoons ground cumin

Finely grated zest of 1 lemon

2 tablespoons finely chopped fresh parsley

2 tablespoons finely chopped fresh oregano

4 tomatoes, cut into wedges

Mixed salad greens, to serve

Preparation: 15 minutes

Cooking: 6–8 minutes

Serves: 4–6

Level: 1

FILLET STEAK WITH SPICY VEGETABLES

Cook the potatoes in a large saucepan of boiling water until tender, 10–15 minutes. • After 7 minutes, add the green beans and sugar snap peas. • Cook until tender, about 3–5 minutes. • Drain well. • Sauté the steaks in 1 tablespoon of oil for about 4 minutes on each side, or until cooked to your liking. • Season with salt and pepper. • Slice the steak into thin strips. • Mix the remaining oil, red wine vinegar, garlic, mustard, and sugar in a small bowl. • Arrange the steak, potatoes, green beans, sugar snap peas, olives, chile, parsley, and tomatoes in a large salad bowl. Drizzle with the dressing and toss gently. • Serve hot.

1	pound (500 g) new potatoes, quartered
4	ounces (125 g) green beans
4	ounces (125 g) sugar snap peas (mangetout)
1	pound (500 g) fillet steak
1/2	cup (125 ml) extra-virgin olive oil
	Salt and freshly ground black pepper
1/4	cup (60 ml) red wine vinegar
1	clove garlic, finely chopped
2	teaspoons mustard
1	teaspoon sugar
3/4	cup (75 g) stuffed green olives
1/2	fresh red chile, seeded and finely chopped
1	tablespoon finely chopped fresh parsley
2	tomatoes, diced

Preparation: 10 minutes
Cooking: 20 minutes

Serves: 4
Level: 1

PORK BURGERS WITH POTATO SALAD

Cook the potatoes in a large saucepan of boiling water until tender, 10–15 minutes. • Drain well and let cool. • Meanwhile, mix the onion, ground pork, eggs, flour, and milk in a large bowl. Season with salt and pepper. • Form the mixture into 12 patties. • Sauté the pork burgers in the oil and butter in a large frying pan over medium-high heat until golden, about 8 minutes, turning from time to time. • Mix the potatoes with the scallions, mayonnaise, lemon juice, and mustard in a large bowl. • Serve the pork burgers hot with the potato salad and beets.

1	pound (500 g) new potatoes, quartered
1	onion, finely chopped
1	pound (500 g) ground (minced) pork
2	large eggs, lightly beaten
1/4	cup (30 g) all-purpose (plain) flour
1/4	cup (60 ml) milk
	Salt and freshly ground black pepper
2	tablespoons extra-virgin olive oil
2	tablespoons butter
2	scallions (green onions), thinly sliced
1/3	cup (90 ml) mayonnaise
1	tablespoon freshly squeezed lemon juice
2	teaspoons mustard
1	(15-ounce/450-g) can beets (beetroot), drained and sliced

Preparation: 15 minutes
Cooking: 15 minutes

Serves: 4–6
Level: 1

GRILLED PORK WITH BEAN SALAD

Mix the beans, tomatoes, feta, oregano, and 1 tablespoon of oil in a large bowl. Season with salt and pepper. • Place a grill pan over medium-high heat. • Drizzle the pork with the remaining oil. Season with salt and pepper. • Grill the pork until cooked, 4–5 minutes each side. • Arrange the pork on serving plates. • Top with the bean salad. • Serve hot with the lemon wedges and tzatziki.

1   (14-ounce/400-g) can cannellini beans, drained and rinsed

2   tomatoes, diced

4   ounces (125 g) feta cheese, crumbled

1   tablespoon dried oregano

2   tablespoons extra-virgin olive oil

Salt and freshly ground black pepper

4   pork loin steaks

1   lemon, cut into wedges, to serve

Tzatziki, to serve

Preparation: 15 minutes
Cooking: 6–8 minutes

Serves: 4
Level: 1

■■■ Tzatziki is a yogurt-based Greek sauce. It is available in some Greek delicatessens or can easily be made at home by mixing Greek yogurt, cucumber, mint, garlic, lemon juice, and olive oil.

PORK WITH SAGE AND LEMON

Sauté the sage in the oil in a large frying pan over medium-high heat for about 2 minutes, until crisp. • Remove the sage from the pan and drain on paper towels. • Sauté the pork in the oil in the same pan until cooked, about 4 minutes on each side. • Remove from the pan and set aside. • Decrease the heat to low. • Add the butter, garlic, chicken stock, and asparagus. • Bring to a boil and simmer until the asparagus is tender, about 3 minutes. • Stir in the lemon juice and season with salt and pepper. • Remove the asparagus with a slotted spoon and arrange on serving plates. • Top with the pork and drizzle with the pan juices. • Garnish with the lemon zest and sage leaves. • Serve hot.

6	leaves fresh sage
2	tablespoons extra-virgin olive oil
4	pork loin steaks
2	tablespoons butter
2	cloves garlic, finely chopped
1/4	cup (60 ml) chicken stock
1	pound (500 g) asparagus, trimmed
	Finely grated zest and juice of 1 lemon
	Salt and freshly ground black pepper

Preparation: 10 minutes
Cooking: 13 minutes

Serves: 4
Level: 1

PORK MARSALA

Cook the potatoes in a large saucepan of boiling water until tender, 10–15 minutes. • Drain well and return to the pan. • Add 2 tablespoons of butter and the milk. Mash until smooth. Season with salt and pepper. • Meanwhile, dust the pork steaks with the flour. • Sauté the pork in 1 tablespoon of oil and the remaining butter in a large frying pan over medium heat until cooked, about 4 minutes on each side. • Remove from the pan and set aside. • Sauté the leek in the remaining oil in the same pan over medium heat until softened, about 3 minutes. • Add the Marsala. Simmer for about 2 minutes until slightly reduced. • Decrease the heat to low. Stir in the cream. Season with salt and pepper. • Return the pork to the pan and cook for 2 minutes. • Serve the pork hot with the mashed potato and broccoli.

1	pound (500 g) potatoes, peeled and diced
1/4	cup (60 g) butter
1/4	cup (60 ml) milk
	Salt and freshly ground black pepper
1 1/2	pounds (750 g) pork loin steaks
1/4	cup (30 g) all-purpose (plain) flour
1/4	cup (60 ml) extra-virgin olive oil
1	leek, halved lengthwise and thinly sliced
1/2	cup (125 ml) Marsala wine or dry sherry
1/2	cup (125 ml) light (single) cream
	Steamed broccoli, to serve

Preparation: 10 minutes
Cooking: 25–30 minutes

Serves: 4
Level: 1

LAMB NOISETTES WITH SUN-DRIED TOMATOES

Preheat the oven to 475°F (250°C/gas 9).
• Arrange the potatoes in a single layer
in a large roasting dish. • Drizzle with
1 tablespoon of oil and toss well. Season
with salt and pepper. • Bake for about
20 minutes until golden and tender.
• Meanwhile, place the lamb noisettes
down on a clean surface. • Use a sharp
knife to open up a pocket in each of the
noisettes. Stuff with the garlic, tomatoes,
and some of the arugula. • Sauté the
lamb in the remaining oil in a large
frying pan until cooked, about 3 minutes
on each side. • Serve the lamb with
the roasted potatoes and the
remaining arugula.

1^1/$_4$ **pounds (600 g) new potatoes, quartered**

2 **tablespoons extra-virgin olive oil**

Salt and freshly ground black pepper

4 **lamb noisettes, about 1^1/$_2$ pounds (750 g) total**

1 **clove garlic, finely chopped**

^{3}/$_4$ **cup (150 g) sun-dried tomatoes, packed in oil, drained**

1 **bunch arugula (rocket)**

Preparation: 10 minutes
Cooking: 20 minutes

Serves: 4
Level: 2

GREEK LAMB CHOPS

Mix $1/4$ cup (60 g) of oil, 2 tablespoons of lemon juice, garlic, and oregano in a small bowl. Season with salt and pepper. • Add the lamb to the mixture and coat well. • Mix the cucumber, tomatoes, onion, feta, and olives in a bowl. • Season with salt and pepper. Drizzle with the remaining oil and lemon juice. • Toss well. • Place a grill pan over medium-high heat. • Grill the lamb until cooked to your liking, about 4 minutes on each side. • Serve the lamb hot with the salad and pita bread.

$1/3$ cup (90 ml) extra-virgin olive oil

$1/4$ cup (60 ml) freshly squeezed lemon juice

2 cloves garlic, finely chopped

2 teaspoons dried oregano

Salt and freshly ground black pepper

12 lamb chops, trimmed

1 small cucumber, diced

2 tomatoes, diced

$1/2$ small onion, finely chopped

2 ounces (60 g) feta cheese, crumbled

$1/3$ cup (30 g) kalamata olives

Pita bread, to serve

Preparation: 15 minutes
Cooking: 8 minutes

Serves: 4
Level: 1

VEAL WITH BEAN SALAD

Mix the lemon juice, chives, garlic, and 1/4 cup (60 ml) of oil in a small bowl. Season with salt. • Combine the arugula, beans, tomatoes, and basil in a large bowl. • Drizzle with the dressing and toss well. • Dust the veal with the flour, shaking off the excess. • Fry the veal in the remaining oil in a large frying pan over medium-high heat for about 4 minutes on each side. • Transfer the veal to a serving plate and keep warm. • Add the stock to the cooking juices in the pan. Cook over high heat for 2 minutes. • Stir in the butter. • Cook over medium heat until slightly thickened, about 2 minutes. • Pour the sauce over the veal and serve with the bean salad.

1/4 cup (60 ml) freshly squeezed lemon juice

1 tablespoon finely chopped fresh chives

2 cloves garlic, finely chopped

1/3 cup (90 ml) extra-virgin olive oil

Salt

4 ounces (125 g) arugula (rocket)

1 (14-ounce/400-g) can white kidney beans, drained and rinsed

8 large tomatoes, finely chopped

4 tablespoons torn fresh basil

4 veal scallops (escalopes)

1/2 cup (75 g) all-purpose (plain) flour

1/2 cup (125 ml) vegetable stock

1/4 cup (60 g) butter, diced

Preparation: 10 minutes
Cooking: 12 minutes

Serves: 4
Level: 1

261

VEAL SALTIMBOCCA

Sauté the potatoes in 2 tablespoons of oil in a large frying pan over medium heat until tender and golden, about 10 minutes. • Season with salt and pepper. • Fry the veal in 2 tablespoons of butter and the remaining oil in a large frying pan over medium-high heat for about 2 minutes on each side. • Preheat the broiler (grill). • Transfer the veal to a large roasting pan. Top each scallop with the fontina, prosciutto, and sage leaves. Secure with toothpicks. • Broil for about 2 minutes, until the cheese melts. • Melt the remaining butter in the frying pan in which you cooked the veal. • Add the stock and wine. Bring to a boil. • Simmer over low heat until the sauce reduces slightly, about 2 minutes. • Stir in the chopped sage. • Serve the veal with the potatoes and pan juices.

$1^1/4$ pounds (600 g) potatoes, thinly sliced

$1/4$ cup (60 ml) extra-virgin olive oil

Salt and freshly ground black pepper

4 veal scallops (escalopes)

$1/4$ cup (60 g) butter

1 cup (125 g) freshly grated fontina cheese

8 slices prosciutto (Parma ham)

12 leaves fresh sage + 1 tablespoon coarsely chopped

$1/4$ cup (60 ml) beef stock

$1/4$ cup (60 ml) dry white wine

Preparation: 15 minutes
Cooking: 15 minutes

Serves: 4
Level: 1

VEGETABLES

POTATO, EGGPLANT, AND SPINACH CURRY

Bring a large saucepan of salted water to a boil. • Add the rice and cook over medium heat until tender, 10–15 minutes. • Drain well and set aside. • Meanwhile, sauté the onion and garlic in the oil in a large saucepan over medium-low heat for about 3 minutes, until softened. • Stir in the curry paste, tomatoes, vegetable stock, potatoes, and eggplant. • Bring to a boil. • Cover and simmer over low heat until the vegetables are tender, about 15 minutes. • Add the spinach. Cook until wilted, about 2 minutes. • Stir in the cilantro and season with salt and pepper. • Serve the curry hot with the rice.

2	cups (400 g) basmati rice
1	onion, thinly sliced
2	cloves garlic, finely chopped
1	tablespoon canola oil
1/4	cup (60 ml) korma curry paste
1 1/2	cups (375 ml) chopped tomatoes
1/2	cup (125 ml) vegetable stock
3	potatoes, peeled and diced
1	large eggplant (aubergine), diced
5	ounces (150 g) baby spinach leaves
2	tablespoons finely chopped fresh cilantro
	Salt and freshly ground black pepper

■■■ *Korma curry paste is available wherever Indian foods are sold and online.*

Preparation: 10 minutes
Cooking: 20 minutes

Serves: 4
Level: 1

THAI VEGETABLE GREEN CURRY

Bring a large saucepan of salted water to a boil. • Add the rice and cook over medium heat until tender, 10–15 minutes. • Drain well. • Meanwhile, place a wok over high heat. • When it is very hot, stir-fry the garlic and onion in the oil until softened, about 2 minutes. • Stir in the curry paste. • Cook until aromatic, about 30 seconds. • Add the zucchini, squash, mushrooms, coconut milk, vegetable stock, brown sugar, and fish sauce. • Decrease the heat to low. • Cover and simmer until the vegetables are tender, about 10 minutes. • Garnish with the cilantro. • Serve the curry hot with the rice.

2 cups (400 g) jasmine rice

2 cloves garlic, finely chopped

1 onion, thinly sliced

1 tablespoon peanut oil

1/4 cup (60 ml) Thai green curry paste

2 zucchini (courgettes), thinly sliced

12 baby yellow summer squash, quartered

8 ounces (250 g) mushrooms, thinly sliced

1 cup (250 ml) coconut milk

1/4 cup (60 ml) vegetable stock

2 teaspoons brown sugar

1 tablespoon Asian fish sauce

3 tablespoons fresh cilantro (coriander)

Preparation: 10 minutes

Cooking: 15 minutes

Serves: 4

Level: 1

SPICY BEAN STEW

Bring a large saucepan of salted water to a boil. • Add the rice and cook over medium heat until tender, 10–15 minutes. • Drain well. • Meanwhile, sauté the onion, bell peppers, garlic, and chiles in the oil in a large frying pan over medium heat until softened, about 3 minutes. • Add the cumin and paprika. Cook until aromatic, about 30 seconds. • Stir in the carrot, tomatoes, and the bean mix. Season with salt and pepper. • Bring to a boil. • Cover and simmer over low heat until the sauce reduces slightly, 10–12 minutes. • Stir in the cilantro. • Garnish with the cilantro and serve hot with the rice.

Preparation: 10 minutes
Cooking: 15 minutes

Serves: 4–6
Level: 1

2	cups (400 g) jasmine rice
1	onion, thinly sliced
1	small red bell pepper (capsicum), seeded and thinly sliced
1	small green bell pepper (capsicum), seeded and thinly sliced
2	cloves garlic, finely chopped
1–2	green chiles, seeded and finely chopped
1	tablespoon extra-virgin olive oil
1	teaspoon ground cumin
1	teaspoon paprika
1	carrot, diced
2	(14-ounce/400-g) cans tomatoes, with juice
1	(14-ounce/400-g) can white kidney beans
1	(14-ounce/400-g) can red kidney beans
	Salt and freshly ground black pepper
	Cilantro (coriander) to garnish

POTATOES STUFFED WITH BEANS

Pierce the potatoes four times with a skewer. • Microwave on high power for 4 minutes. • Turn the potatoes over and microwave for 4 minutes more. • Remove the potatoes from the microwave and wrap in aluminum foil. • Let stand for 5 minutes. • Cut each potato in half. • Carefully scoop out the flesh and coarsely mash it. • Meanwhile, sauté the onion, garlic, and bacon in the oil in a large frying pan over medium heat until softened, about 3 minutes. • Mix the onion mixture into the mashed potato. Stir in the tomatoes and beans. • Spoon the mixture into the potato shells. • Place the potatoes on a baking sheet. • Sprinkle with the cheddar. • Preheat the broiler (grill). • Broil the potatoes for about 3 minutes, until the cheese melts. • Serve hot.

8	medium potatoes
1	red onion, finely chopped
2	cloves garlic, finely chopped
3	slices bacon, coarsely chopped
2	tablespoons extra-virgin olive oil
2	tomatoes, coarsely chopped
1	(14-ounce/400-g) cannellini beans, drained and rinsed
1	cup (125 g) freshly grated cheddar cheese

Preparation: 15 minutes
Cooking: 15 minutes

Serves: 4
Level: 1

GADO GADO

Combine the satay sauce, coconut milk, lime juice, and kecap manis in a small saucepan. Heat over medium heat until simmering. • Cover and keep warm. • Meanwhile, boil the eggs in a small saucepan of boiling water for 4 minutes. Drain. • Cool the eggs in cold water and peel. • Place the potatoes in a steamer basket over a pan of simmering water. Cover and steam until almost tender, about 5 minutes. • Add the beans and carrots. Cover and steam for 2 minutes. • Add cabbage and bean sprouts. Cover and steam until cabbage just begins to wilt, about 1 minute. • Arrange the steamed vegetables and tomatoes on serving plates. Halve the eggs lengthwise and place on the plates. • Drizzle the vegetables with warm satay mixture. Garnish with the chiles and serve.

■■■ *Kecap manis is a sweetened Indonesian soy sauce. It is available online.*

$1/3$ **cup (90 ml) Thai satay sauce**

$1/3$ **cup (90 ml) coconut milk**

1 **tablespoon freshly squeezed lime juice**

2 **teaspoons kecap manis**

4 **large eggs**

8 **small new potatoes, halved**

5 **ounces (150 g) green beans, topped**

2 **carrots, thickly sliced on the diagonal**

$1/2$ **small medium Chinese cabbage, thickly sliced lengthwise**

1 **cup (100 g) bean sprouts**

2 **medium tomatoes, cut into thick wedges**

Sliced fresh red chiles, to serve

Preparation: 15 minutes

Cooking: 15 minutes

Serves: 4

Level: 1

ROAST BUTTERNUT SQUASH WITH SWEET ORANGE DRESSING

Preheat the oven to 450°F (230°C/gas 8). • Place the squash on a large nonstick baking sheet. Drizzle with the olive oil and season with salt and pepper. • Roast for 15–20 minutes, or until tender. • Meanwhile, to make the dressing, combine the grapeseed oil, vinegar, orange juice, honey, cayenne pepper, salt, and pepper in a saucepan. Stir to combine. • Heat over low heat until warm. • Arrange the spinach, roast squash, and fennel on serving plates. Drizzle with the warm dressing and serve hot.

1³/₄ pounds (800 g) butternut squash or pumpkin, seeded and cut into ¹/₂-inch (1-cm) thick wedges

3 tablespoons extra-virgin olive oil

Salt and freshly ground black pepper

1 tablespoon grapeseed oil

1 tablespoon red wine vinegar

1 tablespoon freshly squeezed orange juice

3 tablespoons honey

Pinch cayenne pepper

Salt and freshly ground black pepper

1 cup (50 g) baby spinach leaves

2 baby fennel bulbs, trimmed and very thinly sliced

Preparation: 10 minutes

Cooking: 15–20 minutes

Serves: 4

Level: 1

POTATO, GREEN BEAN, AND FETA SALAD

Bring a saucepan of salted water to a boil over high heat. • Add the beans and cook until just crisp, 2–3 minutes. Remove with a slotted spoon. Refresh in cold water and drain well. Place in a large bowl. • Add the potatoes to the pan. Boil until just tender, about 10 minutes. Drain. Refresh in cold water. Add the potatoes to the beans in the bowl. • Heat a small frying pan over medium heat. • Add 2 teaspoons of oil and heat until hot. • Add the walnuts and cook, stirring from time to time, until golden, about 2 minutes. • Add the walnuts and feta to the beans and potatoes in the bowl. • To make the dressing, combine the remaining oil, balsamic vinegar, salt, and pepper in a screw-top jar. Shake well to combine. • Pour the dressing over potato mixture and gently toss to combine.

8	ounces (250 g) green beans, topped
1	pound (500 g) new potatoes, scrubbed and halved
1/4	cup (60 ml) extra-virgin olive oil
1/2	cup (80 g) walnuts, coarsely chopped
4	ounces (125 g) feta cheese, sliced
1	tablespoon balsamic vinegar
	Salt and freshly ground black pepper

Preparation: 15 minutes
Cooking: 15 minutes

Serves: 4
Level: 1

SWEET AND SOUR MUSHROOMS

Heat a wok over high heat. • Add the oil and heat until hot. • Add onion and stir-fry for 1 minute. • Add celery and bell pepper. Stir-fry for 1 minute. • Add the mushrooms and stir-fry for 2 minutes. • Add the sweet and sour sauce and soy sauce. Stir-fry until the sauce is hot, 1–2 minutes. • Add the tomatoes and toss well. • Serve hot with the jasmine rice and scallions.

2   tablespoons peanut oil

1   red onion, cut into thin wedges

2   stalks celery, thinly sliced diagonally

1   red bell pepper (capsicum), halved, seeded and coarsely chopped

12 ounces (350 g) button mushrooms, halved

1   cup (250 ml) sweet and sour sauce

2   teaspoons soy sauce

4   ounces (125 g) cherry tomatoes, halved lengthwise

Steamed jasmine rice, to serve

Shredded scallions (green onions), to serve

Preparation: 15 minutes

Cooking: 5 minutes

Serves: 4

Level: 1

SPICED CRUMBED EGGPLANT WITH FETA

Combine the bread crumbs with the cumin and coriander in a small bowl. Season with salt and freshly ground black pepper. • Dip the eggplant into the egg. Coat evenly in spiced bread crumbs, pressing the crumbs onto the eggplant. • Heat the oil in a large frying pan over medium-high heat. • Fry the eggplant in batches, until golden, 2–3 minutes per side. • Arrange the arugula on serving plates. Top with eggplant and feta. Serve hot with the hummus, if liked.

1	cup (150 g) fine dry bread crumbs
1	teaspoon ground cumin
1	teaspoon ground coriander
	Salt and freshly ground black pepper
10	baby eggplants (aubergine), halved lengthwise
1	large egg, lightly beaten
1	cup (250 ml) extra-virgin olive oil
1	bunch arugula (rocket)
4	ounces (125 g) feta cheese, very thinly sliced
	Hummus, to serve (optional)

 Preparation: 15 minutes
Cooking: 12 minutes

Serves: 4
Level: 1

SWEET POTATO, ZUCCHINI, AND GARBANZO BEAN STEW

Heat the oil in a large deep frying pan over medium-high heat. • Sauté the onion and garlic until softened, about 3 minutes. • Add the cumin. Cook for 1 minute, until fragrant. • Add the cinnamon stick, saffron, tomatoes, and vegetable stock. Cover and bring to a boil. • Add the sweet potato, zucchini, and garbanzo beans. Reduce the heat to medium-low and simmer until tender, 15–20 minutes. • Stir in the parsley and season with salt and pepper. • Remove the cinnamon stick. Serve hot with the couscous.

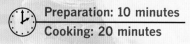

Preparation: 10 minutes
Cooking: 20 minutes

Serves: 4
Level: 1

3   tablespoons extra-virgin olive oil

1   onion, finely chopped

2   cloves garlic, finely chopped

2   teaspoons ground cumin

1   cinnamon stick

1/4 teaspoon saffron threads, soaked in 1 tablespoon water

2   (14-ounce/400-g) cans diced tomatoes, with juice

1/2 cup (125 ml) vegetable stock

1 1/2 pounds (800 g) orange sweet potato (kumara), peeled and diced

2   zucchini (courgettes), sliced

1   (14-ounce/400-g) can garbanzo beans (chick-peas), drained and rinsed

1/3 cup coarsely chopped flat leaf parsley

Salt and freshly ground black pepper

Couscous, to serve

CABBAGE, BROCCOLI, AND BABY CORN STIR-FRY

286

Heat a wok over high heat. Add the oil.
• Add the onion and stir-fry until tender, about 2 minutes. • Add the curry paste and stir-fry until fragrant, about 1 minute.
• Add the coconut milk. Stir until the oil separates. • Add the broccoli, corn, and fish sauce. Cover and bring to a boil.
• Add the cabbage and tofu. • Stir-fry until the cabbage just wilts, 1–2 minutes.
• Add the lime juice and toss gently.
• Spoon into serving bowls. Top with the cucumber and cilantro. • Serve hot with the rice.

1	tablespoon peanut oil
1	onion, cut into thin wedges
1/4	cup (60 ml) Thai green curry paste
1	cup (250 ml) coconut milk
8	ounces (250 g) broccoli, cut into small florets
8	ounces (250 g) baby corn, halved
1	tablespoon Asian fish sauce
1/4	Chinese cabbage, trimmed and shredded
12	ounces (350 g) firm bean curd, cut into 1-inch (2.5-cm) cubes
1	tablespoon freshly squeezed lime juice
1	small cucumber, cut into matchsticks
1/2	cup cilantro (coriander) sprigs
	Steamed jasmine rice, to serve

Preparation: 15 minutes
Cooking: 12 minutes

Serves: 4
Level: 1

SWEET CORN FRITTERS WITH AVOCADO SALSA

To prepare the salsa, combine the avocados, lime juice, 1 tablespoon of cilantro, and Tabasco sauce in a bowl. Season with salt and pepper. Stir to combine. Set aside. • To prepare the corn fritters, put the flour in a large bowl. • Beat the egg and milk in small bowl • Whisk the egg mixture into the flour until smooth. Set aside for 5 minutes. • Add the corn, scallions, and cilantro to the egg batter. Season with salt and pepper. Stir to combine. • Heat the oil in a large nonstick frying pan over medium-high heat. • Add $1/3$ cup of batter for each fritter and fry until golden and cooked through, 2–3 minutes per side. Drain on paper towels while you cook the remaining batter. • Serve the fritters hot with the avocado salsa and garnished with lime wedges.

Salsa

2	ripe avocados, peeled, halved, pitted, and chopped
3	tablespoons freshly squeezed lime juice
1	tablespoon chopped cilantro (coriander)
	Dash of Tabasco
	Salt and freshly ground black pepper

Corn Fritters

$2/3$	cup (100 g) self-rising flour
1	large egg, lightly beaten
$2/3$	cup (150 ml) milk
1	(14-ounce/400-g) can corn, drained
4	scallions (green onions), thinly sliced
1	tablespoon chopped cilantro (coriander)
1	cup (250 ml) vegetable oil, to fry
	Lime wedges, to serve

Preparation: 15 minutes

Cooking: 15 minutes

Serves: 4

Level: 1

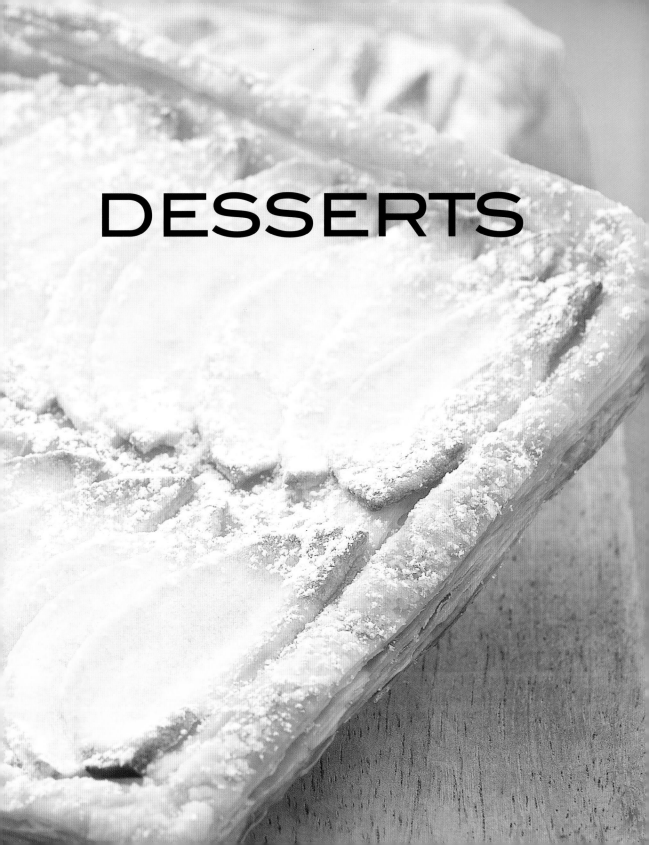

DESSERTS

CHOCOLATE CHIP PUDDINGS

To prepare the puddings, preheat the oven to 350°F (180°C/gas 4). • Butter four $3/4$-cup (180-ml) ramekins or mini soufflé dishes. Arrange on a baking sheet. • Sift the flour, cocoa, and salt into a large bowl. • Stir in the brown sugar. • Mix in the butter, milk, and egg until well combined. • Stir in $1/4$ cup (30 g) of chocolate chips. • Spoon the mixture evenly into the ramekins and sprinkle with the remaining chocolate chips. • To prepare the sauce: Mix the brown sugar and cocoa in a small bowl. • Sprinkle the mixture evenly over the ramekins. • Gently pour over the boiling water over the back of a spoon, dividing it evenly among the ramekins. • Bake for about 20 minutes, until set.
• Serve warm.

Puddings

1 cup (150 g) self-rising flour

1 tablespoon unsweetened cocoa powder

$1/8$ teaspoon salt

$1/3$ cup (50 g) firmly packed dark brown sugar

$1/4$ cup (60 g) butter, melted

$1/3$ cup (90 ml) milk

1 large egg, lightly beaten

$1/3$ cup (50 g) dark chocolate chips

Sauce

$1/4$ cup (50 g) firmly packed dark brown sugar

2 teaspoons unsweetened cocoa powder

$3/4$ cup (180 ml) water, boiling

 Preparation: 10 minutes
Cooking: 20 minutes

Serves: 4
Level: 1

PASSIONFRUIT AND APRICOT SOUFFLÉS

Preheat the oven to 350°F (180°C/gas 4).
• Butter four 3/4-cup (180-ml) ramekins
or mini soufflé dishes. Dust each ramekin
with 1 teaspoon of superfine sugar.
Arrange on a baking sheet. • Drain the
apricots, reserving the liquid. • Put the
apricots in a food processor and process
until smooth. • Mix $\frac{1}{2}$ cup (125 ml) of
the apricot purée with the passionfruit
pulp. • Mix the remaining apricot
purée with $\frac{1}{4}$ cup (60 ml) of the
reserved liquid. • Set aside. • Beat the
egg whites and salt in a large bowl with
an electric mixer at high speed until soft
peaks form. • Gradually add the
remaining superfine sugar, beating until
stiff peaks form. • Use a large rubber
spatula to gently fold in the apricot and
passionfruit mixture. • Spoon the mixture
evenly into the ramekins. • Bake for
10–12 minutes, until risen. • Dust with
the confectioners' sugar. Serve with the
apricot sauce on the side.

$\frac{1}{2}$ cup (100 g)
superfine (caster)
sugar

1 (14-ounce/400-g)
can apricot halves

Pulp of 2
passionfruit

3 large egg whites

$\frac{1}{8}$ teaspoon salt

Confectioners'
(icing) sugar, to dust

Preparation: 15 minutes
Cooking: 10–12 minutes

Serves: 4
Level: 1

APPLE PASTRIES

Preheat the oven to 400°F (200°C/ gas 6). • Line a baking sheet with parchment paper. • Cut each pastry sheet into 4 squares. • Arrange 4 squares of pastry on the prepared sheet. • Brush lightly with water. • Top with the remaining pastry squares and press together lightly. • Use a sharp knife to cut a $1/2$-inch (1 cm) border around the edge. • Arrange the apple slices on top of the pastry. • Brush with the melted butter and sprinkle evenly with the superfine sugar. • Bake for 15–20 minutes, until golden and puffed.
• Dust with the confectioners' sugar.

2 sheets frozen puff pastry, thawed

3 apples, peeled, cored, and thinly sliced

2 tablespoons butter, melted

1 tablespoon superfine (caster) sugar

Confectioners' (icing) sugar, to dust

Preparation: 10 minutes
Cooking: 15–20 minutes

Serves: 4
Level: 1

BOOZY STRAWBERRIES

Mix the sugar, orange zest and juice, and liqueur in a small saucepan over medium heat. • Cook, stirring, until the sugar dissolves, about 3 minutes. • Let cool completely. • Arrange the strawberries in individual serving bowls. • Drizzle with the syrup and sprinkle with the almonds. • Serve with the cream on the side.

1/4 **cup (50 g) superfine (caster) sugar**

Finely grated zest and freshly squeezed juice of 1 orange

2 **tablespoons orange liqueur**

1 **pound (500 g) strawberries, hulled and quartered**

1/4 **cup (40 g) slivered almonds, toasted**

Heavy (double) cream, to serve

Preparation: 10 minutes
Cooking: 4 minutes

Serves: 4
Level: 1

SPICED POACHED PEARS

Mix the water, superfine sugar, lemon juice, orange zest, and cinnamon stick in a large saucepan over high heat. • Use a teaspoon to scrape seeds from the vanilla pod into the pan. • Add the scraped pod to the pan. • Bring to a boil, stirring from time to time. • Decrease the heat to medium. • Cook, uncovered, until the volume has reduced by one-third, 8–10 minutes. • Add the pears to the syrup. • Cover and simmer until tender, 5–8 minutes. • Arrange the warm pears in individual serving bowls. • Spoon over the syrup and serve with the cream.

2   cups (500 ml) water

1   cup (200 g) superfine (caster) sugar

1   tablespoon freshly squeezed lemon juice

1   piece orange zest

1   cinnamon stick

1   vanilla pod, halved lengthwise

4   large firm-ripe pears, quartered lengthwise and cored

Heavy (double) cream, to serve

Preparation: 10 minutes
Cooking: 13–18 minutes

Serves: 4
Level: 1

CHOCOLATE MOUSSE

Melt the chocolate with the cream in a double boiler over barely simmering water. • Meanwhile, beat the egg yolk in a small bowl with an electric mixer at high speed until light and creamy. • Stir the beaten yolk into the chocolate mixture. Cook until the mixture registers 160°F (80°C) on an instant-read thermometer. • Set aside. • With a mixer at high speed, beat the egg white in a small bowl placed over a pan of barely simmering water until soft peaks form. • Gradually add the superfine sugar, beating until stiff peaks form. • Use a large rubber spatula to fold the beaten white into the chocolate mixture. • Spoon the mixture into four $1/2$-cup (125-ml) ramekins. • Freeze for about 20 minutes, until just set. • Sprinkle with the chopped peanut candy and serve.

8   ounces (250 g) semisweet (dark) chocolate, coarsely chopped

$3/4$ cup (180 ml) single (light) cream

1   tablespoon superfine (caster) sugar

2   tablespoons coffee liqueur

1   large egg, separated

$1/2$ cup (90 g) chocolate coated peanuts, coarsely chopped

Preparation: 10 minutes + 20 minutes to freeze

Serves: 4
Level: 1

QUICK TIRAMISU

Mix the coffee and Marsala in a shallow dish. • Beat the cream cheese and confectioners' sugar with an electric mixer at high speed in a large bowl until creamy. • Use a large rubber spatula to fold the mascarpone cheese into the cream cheese mixture. • Dip the ladyfingers in the coffee mixture and arrange them standing upright in four individual serving glasses. • Spoon the cream cheese mixture into the dishes and sprinkle with the chocolate. • Chill for 15 minutes, or until ready to serve.

1/2 cup (125 ml) strong black coffee, cooled

2 tablespoons Marsala or sweet sherry

1 cup (250 g) cream cheese, softened

3 tablespoons confectioners' (icing) sugar

1 cup (250 ml) mascarpone cheese

12 small ladyfingers (sponge fingers)

Finely grated chocolate, to garnish

Preparation: 10 minutes + 15 minutes to chill

Serves: 4
Level: 1

CHOCOLATE FUDGE AND AMARETTI SUNDAES

Melt the butter in a medium frying pan over medium heat. • Add the brown sugar, cream, and cocoa powder. • Simmer until slightly reduced, about 5 minutes. • Let cool slightly. • Layer the amaretti cookies, peanuts, ice cream, and fudge sauce in individual sundae glasses. • Serve at once.

$1/3$ cup (90 g) butter

$1/2$ cup (100 g) firmly packed dark brown sugar

$1/2$ cup (125 ml) heavy (double) cream

2 tablespoons unsweetened cocoa powder

$3/4$ cup (90 g) amaretti cookies, crushed

$1/2$ cup (90 g) chocolate-coated peanuts, coarsely chopped

1 quart (1 liter) vanilla ice cream

Preparation: 15 minutes

Cooking: 5 minutes

Serves: 4
Level: 1

BAKED PEACHES WITH MERINGUE

Preheat the oven to 350°F (180°C/gas 4).
• Place the peaches, cut side up, in a
shallow baking dish. • Beat the egg
whites in a large bowl with an electric
mixer at high speed until soft peaks
form. • Gradually add the superfine
sugar, beating until stiff, glossy peaks
form. • Pipe the meringue on top
of the peaches. • Bake for about
10 minutes, until lightly browned.
• Dust with the confectioners' sugar
and serve hot.

8   **canned peach
halves, drained**

2   **large egg whites (at
room temperature)**

$1/4$ **cup (50 g) superfine
(caster) sugar**

   **Confectioners'
(icing) sugar, to dust**

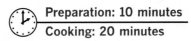

Preparation: 10 minutes
Cooking: 20 minutes

Serves: 4
Level: 1

BRANDY SNAPS WITH MOCHA MASCARPONE

Beat the mascarpone and confectioners' sugar in a small bowl until smooth. • Mix the coffee granules, cocoa, and boiling water in a small bowl. • Use a large rubber spatula to stir the coffee mixture into the mascarpone mixture. • Place one cookie on each serving plate. Top with one-third of the mascarpone mixture. Repeat the layering twice, finishing with a cookie. • Dust with cocoa and serve at once.

1   cup (250 g) mascarpone cheese

3   tablespoons confectioners' (icing) sugar

1   tablespoon instant coffee granules

2   teaspoons unsweetened cocoa powder

1   tablespoon boiling water

16 brandy snap cookies
    Cocoa powder, to dust

 Preparation: 10 minutes

Serves: 4
Level: 1

STRAWBERRY AND COCONUT DESSERT

Toast the coconut in a large frying pan until golden, about 5 minutes. • Mix the orange juice and passionfruit pulp in a small bowl. • Beat the cream in a large bowl with an electric mixer at high speed until soft peaks form. • Use a large rubber spatula to fold half the toasted coconut into the cream.
• Arrange half the cake in the bottom of a medium shallow dish. • Sprinkle with half the orange mixture and top with half the coconut cream. •
Repeat the layering, finishing with the cream. • Arrange the strawberries on top.
• Sprinkle with remaining coconut and serve at once.

$3/4$ **cup (90 g) shredded coconut**

Juice of 2 oranges

Pulp of 2 passionfruits

$1^1/2$ **cups (375 ml) heavy (double) cream**

8 **$1/2$-inch (1-cm) thick slices pound cake or Madeira cake, crusts removed**

8 **ounces (250 g) strawberries, hulled and thinly sliced**

Preparation: 20 minutes
Cooking: 5 minutes

Serves: 4
Level: 1

CHOCOLATE TARTS

Preheat the oven to 400°F (200°C/ gas 6). • Combine the butter, chocolate, and superfine sugar in a medium saucepan over low heat. • Cook, stirring constantly, for 5 minutes. • Remove from the heat. Stir in the egg. • Lightly butter four individual tart pans. • Cut the pastry into four rounds to fit the tart pans. Line the pans with the pastry. • Spoon the chocolate mixture into each tart case. • Bake for 12–15 minutes, until set. • Dust with the confectioners' sugar and serve at once.

$1/4$ **cup (60 g) butter, cut up**

4 **ounces (125 g) dark chocolate, coarsely chopped**

2 **tablespoons superfine (caster) sugar**

1 **large egg, lightly beaten**

1 **sheet frozen puff pastry, thawed**

Confectioners' (icing) sugar, to dust

Preparation: 10 minutes
Cooking: 17–20 minutes

Serves: 4
Level: 2

Index